Teaching for Thinking Today

Teaching for Thinking Today

Theory, Strategies, and Activities for the K–8 Classroom

Selma Wassermann

Teachers College, Columbia University
New York and London

Published by Teachers College Press, 1234 Amsterdam Avenue, New York, NY 10027

Library of Congress Cataloging-in-Publication Data

Wassermann, Selma.
    Teaching for thinking today : theory, strategies, and activities for the K–8
  classroom / Selma Wassermann.
        p. cm.
    Includes bibliographical references and index.
    ISBN 978-0-8077-5012-4 (pbk. : alk. paper)
    ISBN 978-0-8077-5013-1 (hardcover : alk. paper)
    1. Thought and thinking—Study and teaching—Activity programs.
  2. Effective teaching. I. Title.
  LB1590.3.W3697 2009
  372.139–dc22   2009020476

ISBN 978-0-8077-5012-4 (paper)
ISBN 978-0-8077-5013-1 (cloth)

Printed on acid-free paper
Manufactured in the United States of America

16   15   14   13   12   11   10   09   8   7   6   5   4   3   2   1

Contents

PART III
CLASSROOM APPLICATIONS:
THINKING ACTIVITIES IN THE CURRICULUM AREAS

For Paula,
In a class by herself

The mind is a machine ill suited to desuetude.
The occasional holiday is all very well, but without
the oil of challenge and the heat generated
by effort, the mind rusts and seizes
and is unavailable when needed.
—Laurie R. King, *The Art of Detection*

A good memory is a cheap trick that
creates a deceptive aura of intelligence
around an otherwise ordinary intellect.
—Joe Queenan, "Why I Can't Stop Starting Books"

Preface

It was a warm and sultry day—the kind of weather that the end of September brings, and with it a longing for summer past. I was being taken for a tour around the building before beginning an in-service, after-school workshop for teachers in the district. The classroom doors were open, teachers and children hoping for any cross ventilation that would lower temperatures to a bearable level. Now, close to the end of the school day, there was not a dry face, and sweaty hands clutched pencils to eke out the last answers to the worksheets before the relief of the last bell.

As we approached the Grade 6 class, the teacher beckoned me and invited me into her classroom. With a hunger to know that was palpable, she asked me if I would "show her how to give a lesson in thinking" to her students. I didn't know how to respond to her. How does one "teach" a set of complex skills in a 15-minute lesson as if it were a demonstration of how to make pastry dough? Would that I had a magic wand to make the complex simple, to show and tell, in words and actions that she might immediately understand, the theoretical principles, and the teaching strategies that are woven together to turn a standard lesson into one with an emphasis on thinking. I left her, her frustration feeding mine, and in all these years, her question has haunted me. To make the theoretical principles, strategies, and classroom applications of "teaching for thinking" clear to teachers who wish to use those tools—that seemed to me to be a educational mission worth pursuing, and it is one to which I have given much of my professional life. This book is, finally, a response to that Grade 6 teacher.

There is no question that this is a propitious time for this new book on thinking. We live in turbulent times, and it is very difficult for children to make meaning of what they see and hear all around them. Not only are children being bombarded with massive amounts of data from multimedia sources, but the pace of information flow is faster than ever. "Society's in overdrive everywhere, with no sign of braking" (Gleick, 2000, back cover). "Spin" has become elevated to a new art form; the distortion and manipulation of data make it increasingly difficult even for adults to discern spin from truth.

How, then, are children to interpret the data and make sense of what they see and hear? How are they going to cope with the increase of information and the speed at which it is disseminated? How are teachers to prepare them to take on the challenges and responsibilities they will face as citizens in a democratic society? How will they learn to make wise and informed choices from among the vast numbers of options offered?

The answers to such questions do not lie in the unfortunate and misguided No Child Left Behind legislation of 2001 and the resulting high-stakes testing movement in which children are being drilled in mind-numbing ways to memorize, without thoughtful consideration, a mass of low-level information bytes. Children need time to reflect, to observe, to study, to inquire, and to make intelligent meaning of what is happening all around them. They need to learn to make informed decisions based on data analysis, for without such skills, they are doomed to adult lives as low-paid workers in an economy that has no reward for those who cannot cope with the challenges of solving sophisticated problems that have yet to surface. Without such higher-order skills, their education will have left them bereft, disempowered, and unable to function in this complicated world.

Since the publication of Louis E. Raths's seminal work, *Teaching for Thinking* (Raths, Wassermann, Jonas, & Rothstein, 1986), we have learned much about "teaching for thinking"—especially in our understanding of the relationship between thinking and empowerment, and in the use of activities and discussion strategies that lead to thoughtful examination of issues. *Teaching for Thinking Today* expands on that earlier work and provides new approaches to classroom practice. It includes new and innovative classroom strategies that enable and empower students to think about issues, deepen understanding, and learn about choosing and decision making across virtually all curriculum areas.

Chapters 1 and 2, in Part I, present a theoretical framework of teaching for thinking and link that framework to important educational standards and goals. In Part II, Chapters 3 and 4 describe the kinds of teachers' questions and responses that lead to students' understanding of issues of significance— that is, the big ideas. In Part III, Chapter 5 introduces Chapters 6–9, which offer dozens of examples of how teachers can put an emphasis on thinking skills within the curriculum areas of mathematics, science, language arts, and social studies, in primary, elementary, and middle school classrooms. These activities demonstrate how students gather information, develop understanding of the big ideas of the lessons, and apply these principles in the solving of practical problems. In short, the activities show how the existing classroom curriculum may be tweaked to emphasize higher order thinking skills. Chapters 9 and 10, in Part IV, give suggestions for teachers who wish to embark on a teaching for thinking program, and offer tools for evaluating student progress.

This book was written for all those elementary and middle school teachers—pre-service and in-service—curriculum specialists, and policy makers who are deeply concerned with the urgent need to enable and empower students as thinkers. I have endeavored to make the book "teacher friendly"—written in a jargon-free style that makes it possible for teachers to take from the printed page principles and practices that translate easily into their classrooms. It is dedicated to teachers everywhere who share with me the concern for "making a difference" in the empowerment of children's lives.

The birthing of a book is always a team effort in which members of a behind-the-scenes support system play a key role, from the germination of the ideas to the appearance of the book in print. For their invaluable help in this process, I thank my wonderful editor, Susan Liddicoat, whose consummate skills turn dross into readable prose; my colleagues Maureen and Neil McAllister, for the ongoing dialogue about educational processes; Simon, Lin, Arlo, and Paula, who keep encouraging me to write; and my long-time companion and best friend, Jack, whose patience with a wife-in-progress has no bounds.

PART I

A Case for Theory

CHAPTER 1

What Do We Want for Our Children?

It's snowing. Large fluffy flakes are already covering the school yard with a blanket of white, but the 6th-grade students are oblivious to what is happening outside. They have been engaged in a discussion about racism, centering on the issues surrounding the internment of Japanese Americans in the United States during World War II. In preparation for the discussion, the children viewed the CD-ROM *Presumed Enemies* (Wassermann & Wigmore, 2000), that presented information about Japanese history; the opening of Japan to the West; immigration to the West; the bombing of Pearl Harbor; the conditions that led up to the internment; and the consequences of the unique Executive Order 9066, under which the U. S. Army was given the power to make American citizens of Japanese descent prisoners in their own country. Following the viewing of the CD-ROM, students worked in small study groups to discuss questions that called for examining the overt and hidden agendas behind the issues. Discussions about the ethics and morality of Executive Order 9066 generated very heated debate, as did the government's role in making amends to those interned 40 years later. The teacher, Roger Stevens, planned to use this initial experience to launch a much larger unit on prejudice and injustice not only in the lives of the students, but in the global arena. He was reaching far but considered the issues well worth the time and effort.

For the whole-class discussion that followed the viewing of the CD-ROM and the study groups, Roger had prepared a list of open-ended, higher-order questions to promote further examination of the issues. During the discussion, Roger did not offer an opinion, nor did he judge students' responses as "right" or "wrong." Instead, he used questions to bring about further reflection about the issues, by asking for examples, or for data to support a particular point of view, or for comparisons to be made, or for the kinds of observations that led to a particular belief. At one point he asked a student to offer hypotheses to explain how such a law might have been passed and whether students thought it possible for such a law to be enacted today.

As no one noticed the snow, neither did anyone look at the clock, so that the 3:00 bell took the class and teacher by surprise. No one wanted to leave; there was more to be said! As the students reluctantly rose and went for their coats, Roger said, "We'll pick this up tomorrow. In the meanwhile, don't hesitate to talk about these issues with your parents and get their views on them."

I asked Roger what would happen next, and he was clear that the issues needed more discussion before the choosing of individual or small-group projects, in which students would follow up with background reading and conduct further studies applying what they had learned. Roger had prepared a list of potential projects that students could choose from, but was open to any student-initiated suggestion that was not on his list. Some of the projects on his list included

1. Making a photocollage of the various internment camps in the United States and writing an essay called "Life in the Camps"
2. Designing future immigration laws to include/exclude ethnic groups, identifying the criteria for inclusion and exclusion
3. Investigating the role played by Japanese American soldiers in World War II
4. Writing a short story or a play about Japanese Americans returning home from years of internment and finding signs everywhere saying, "No Japs wanted"
5. Creating a scrapbook that chronicles evidence of ethnic prejudice in governmental policies
6. Compiling a clipping file on events that depict racism
7. Debating between two teams, offering different points of view about the Japanese internment
8. Reenacting a radio broadcast announcing the bombing of Pearl Harbor
9. Locating and interviewing children of former prisoners of an internment camp
10. Developing a computer reenactment of the bombing of Pearl Harbor
11. Making a documentary video or DVD characterizing where injustice is found in a particular community

I followed the students into the hallway after class and asked if I might raise some questions with them. They were eager to tell me what they thought.

I love this class. It has had a big effect on how I learn because if I don't understand something, I feel free to ask. Everyone has a chance to voice their opinion, and I believe this kind of learning helps to bring our class together.

When coming to this class, I had no idea of some of the problems in the world today. Now I feel as if I know a lot more. I can now sit in class and look at different points of view, rather than just seeing my own. Not only have I noticed my change, but my family and friends have too.

This way of teaching has broadened my way of thinking. I have learned to listen to other people and to understand that there are many different interpretations of one topic.

From a textbook you can only get facts, but I found that with this kind of discussion and follow-up, you find out how others feel about certain issues and from these beliefs you can make a judgment.

He [Mr. Stevens] never tells us our ideas are wrong. I've grown more confident in speaking in class and am not afraid to give my opinion. But he does want us to think about what we are saying. (Hah Hah)

As I leave the school I pass through the main entranceway and notice the large poster on the bulletin board facing the entranceway:

Our school goals—what we want all students to become

Caring	Reflective
Good communicators	Risk takers
Inquirers	Principled
Knowledgeable	Thinkers
Open-minded	

I can't help noticing that four out of the nine goals are related to "thinking" and how Roger Stevens is enabling his students to attain these goals.

EDUCATIONAL GOALS FOR THE 21st CENTURY

Educators and other leadership groups have, for at least the past 40 years, identified the need for our students to become more reflective, more critical minded, more effective problem solvers:

> The basics of tomorrow are skills considered to be of a higher level today. These skills include: evaluation and analysis skills; critical thinking; problem solving strategies (including mathematical problem solving); organization and reference skills; synthesis; application; creativity; decision making given incomplete information; and communication skills through a variety of modes. (Education Commission of the States, 1982, p. 165)

The National Leadership Council for Liberal Education and America's Promise, an initiative of the Association of American Colleges and Universities, has worked with business and education leaders to identify the skills that college graduates will need. The learning outcomes encourage the development of advanced skills—the kind that can make use of technologies to push toward creative and innovative reasoning (Lewis, 2007).

It's easy to see why we would wish to aim for such educational goals. The adults we admire most—those who have shown themselves to be successful across a wide spectrum of talents—are people who manifest such abilities in "spades" (see, e.g., Gleick, 1993; Green, 2006; Greenhouse, 2006; Kristof, 2008). Such adults and children are an inspiration to us all. Their self-initiative, resourcefulness, creativity, high degree of problem-solving abilities, and thoughtfulness fill us with admiration. In short, these adults and children are prototypes of the fulfillment of the goals of Roger Stevens's school. Isn't this what we want for all children?

WHAT DOES IT TAKE TO ACHIEVE OUR GOALS?

Jonathan Kozol (2005) conducted a study of 60 schools across the United States where classroom practices have been heavily influenced by the No Child Left Behind law. Standard practices, as reported by Kozol and Jodi Wilgoren (2001) revealed a mind-numbing emphasis on scripted rote-and-drill exercises that lay out explicit rules for stimulus and response, in a Skinnerian mode that is resonant of Orwell. In these classrooms, there is no place for original, creative thinking or any kind of problem solving. The teacher admonishes, "If you do what I tell you to do, how I tell you to do it, when I tell you to do it, you'll get it right. If you don't, you'll get it wrong" (Kozol, 2005, p. 266). Obedience is rewarded, innovation is crushed.

In the classrooms where Kozol gathered his data, from New York to California, the children have silent lunches, and when misbehaving, have silent recess as well. "Zero noise," the teacher demands, as he salutes, in a silent signal, that the children are trained to obey. Teachers' behaviors are scripted; children move through lessons automatically. Intelligent examination of issues, thoughtful inquiry, reflection on ideas—none of these skills have a place in these classrooms. How will these children learn about caring for others? About creativity? About resourcefulness? About self-initiative? About thoughtful reflection? About inquiry? About communication? Where is the encouragement to take a risk? To contribute something *more* to the betterment of the world? How will these children learn to plan a trip? Or write a poem? Or criticize a film? Or make an informed judgment about a candidate for office? Or gather data to support a point of view? Or detect truth from spin in the media? Or program a computer? Or invent an original theory to explain scientific phenomena? Or make good choices that will enrich and satisfy their adult lives?

In a classroom like that of Roger Stevens, where children are given rich and extensive opportunities to think, to develop those critical intelligences that will allow them to function as autonomous, thoughtful adults in a global society, they are already taking the steps toward the kinds of adults we hope our children will become. And, in fact, the data from singular studies have borne this out without equivocation; that is, when children are given opportunities to engage actively, in a curriculum that provides them with opportunities to be problem solvers, to make important decisions, to be creative, to broaden their knowledge base, to communicate their ideas, to consider alternatives, to be thoughtfully reflective, they flourish, not only in school but beyond school as well (Kridel & Bullough, 2007).

Nobody said it was easy. Implementing curriculum experiences that lead to improved critical mindedness in students is not a "walk in the park." A more thoughtful group of students will be more critical and more questioning and less likely to accept things at face value. A more thoughtful group of students will engage in more critical debate and rely less on the teacher as authority. It is much easier to reward those students who sit quietly and don't ask the kinds of questions that make us uncomfortable, who give us the answers we want and accept what we say as truth, who do as they are told. Classrooms run more smoothly when children are conforming and when controversy is muzzled. Solutions give much happier endings than skepticism. Unfortunately, we cannot have it both ways. We cannot have a thinking group of students without the mess that is an adjunct of any productive and creative act. "When there are no crumbs on the floor, there's no food on the table," cautioned my grandmother.

Teaching for thinking demands an openness on the part of teachers that may be light years from their own educational experiences, their teacher training, the classroom texts and workbooks that come neatly packaged and ready for students to fill in all the blanks. It demands an ability to live with uncertainty—for when we think deeply and reflectively about issues, there are rarely any single, right answers, but rather a variety of possible alternatives. It demands stepping away from the comfort of what is known, into the foreign territory of the unknown, and go undaunted, into new explorations. It requires a high tolerance for dissonance and an ability to launch into the "black box" of true inquiry. It is from this fertile soil that the more creative and innovative minds grow. It is what we say we want for all children.

TO KNOW, TO UNDERSTAND, AND TO KNOW HOW

When I was a student in the 6th grade, we were taught the rule about division with fractions: "You just invert the divisor and multiply." This was quite easy to do, provided, of course, a student knew which fraction was the divisor. If the fraction was presented in linear form—for example, ¾ divided by ½—we would know that the divisor, the one to be inverted, was the second fraction. If the fraction was presented in a word problem, we could only guess at which one was to be inverted. When we were tested on division of fractions, and given linear examples, rather than word problems, it was easy to get a good mark. The implication of these good grades was that we "knew" how to divide by fractions. In a very narrow sense, that was true. From a different perspective, it was false. (To my shame, it wasn't until I taught Grade 6 that I taught myself about reciprocals, and hence to *understand* the process of dividing fractions by fractions.)

The words "to know" are much stressed in educational practice, and much classroom effort is tilted toward that goal. We want students to *know*: the correct spellings, the correct answers to test questions, the names of the 50 states, the dates of important world events. But to *know* does not necessarily mean to *understand*. A student can know the names of the letters of the alphabet, but not understand how sounds are blended together to form words. A student may know the mechanics of multiplying double-digit numbers, but not understand that multiplication is an easier way of adding large numbers. Students may know the mnemonic HOMES to remember the initial consonants of the names of the five Great Lakes, but have no idea of what a "great lake" is, or where the lakes are located, or what their social, economic, political, or geographical importance is. Students may know that Columbus sailed the Atlantic Ocean in 1492 and the names of his ships, but have no understanding of the meaning of that voyage and its implications for the larger issues surrounding the "discovery" of the continent to the west of Europe.

For students to "cross the bridge" from merely knowing to understanding, something more has to occur beyond the act of simply absorbing information that enables them to raise their level of knowing to understanding. Students must learn how to put the pieces of the information collected in knowing into a larger framework of understanding. Only a very few, very sophisticated students are able to make their own connections from knowing to understanding—to connect the dots, the bits of information, to see the larger picture. Most students need to be taken "across the bridge" from knowing to understanding; they need to be given specific tasks that enable them to connect the dots. If students are to understand, to get the big ideas, teaching must address the process of building the connection from knowing to understanding. Without their being provided such connections, without those bridges, much of the information learned is lost, and what remains leaves students with a miscellanea of unconnected dots and bereft of their meaning. There is a good reason that students lose 85% of the information "learned" after a 2-month summer vacation.

Knowing how is a further step that takes a student beyond understanding to applying what is known and what is understood, that is, putting ideas into operation. When we are able to apply understanding to the solution of problems we advance further, to the level of knowing how. Teaching students to know how means giving them experiences in applying knowledge to the solution of practical problems. It means, for example, enabling them to apply the principles of electrical circuitry using batteries and bulbs to make a bulb light.

Once again, the inert knowledge of the rudiments of electrical circuitry does not result, automatically, in students knowing how (Bracey, 1998; Shapiro, 1994). In order for them to know how, teaching must provide the further steps so that students may cross yet another bridge to that next level of cognitive development. Teaching to *know* increases students' knowledge base; teaching to *understand* enables them to make meanings from the knowledge gathered; teaching to *know how* enables students to apply knowledge and understanding to the solution of problems. To achieve the goals of all three of these stages of intellectual development, teaching must provide learning experiences in all three areas.

This book is concerned with helping teachers to understand and to use that understanding in the creation of curriculum experiences for their students that emphasize not only knowing, but using information to understand the "big ideas" and to apply them in the solutions of problems—knowing how. This work rests on the premise that if those teaching strategies that enable students to cross the bridge from knowing to understanding and knowing how are made clear, many more teachers will be tempted to use them to further the goals that we all say we want for our students.

MAKING A "CASE" FOR THEORY

The word *theory* has a bad reputation among classroom teachers. "Don't give us that theory stuff. Give us something that works!" is a common reproach in professional workshops. At the mention of the word, teachers tend to shut down or flee in droves. They don't want theory; they are looking for strategies that will help them to deal with the numerous, complex, and often earth-shattering dilemmas they face every day of their teaching lives—not some "pie in the sky" stuff that has little or no relevance to their teaching needs.

Yet sound theory increases teachers' understanding and informs practice. Theory lies at the heart of what professionals do. Without theory to guide us, we act, at best, on intuition, folk wisdom, conventional "truths," or flat-out whim. It is theory that grounds professionals and elevates what they do from mechanics to art.

There are, of course, numerous theories in the sciences (e.g., Copernican theory, germ theory, Snow's theory of the transmission of cholera), the social sciences (e.g., behaviorist theory, operant conditioning theory, Erickson's stages of human development theory, Piaget's theory of intellectual development, Gardner's theory of multiple intelligences), and the humanities (e.g., literary theory, moral theory, Aristotelian theory of tragedy). Good theory has contributed to the thinking of scholars and researchers and has influenced practice in small and large ways.

Theory does not have to be "perfect" in order for us to learn something more about the way the world and the humans in it work, and there is a huge difference between theory that is well grounded in extensive observation and data gathering, and theories that are silly. On the one hand, we simply shrug at "flat-earth theory" and attribute it to a bunch of loonies. Yet, even though Copernican theory was wanting in its explanations about the solar system, other scientists were able to use it as a basis to construct more sophisticated theoretical models.

So that is what theory can do: It can give us a framework to conduct experiments, to make observations, to gather data to determine the extent to which the theory is sound. That is, is the theory supported by further evidence? When there is adequate documentation to support a theory, the theory becomes more credible; and when the data are overwhelming, the theory is elevated to the realm of indisputable knowledge.

In the final analysis, it is teachers who can decide if the educational theory presented to them makes sense. If the theory is sound, if it "fits" in with a teacher's understanding of the educational process, then that teacher may begin to use classroom strategies that are consonant with that theory. When the teaching strategies appear to "work"—that is, when the teacher is able to see results—the theory is supported, allowing the teacher to have more faith in the theory and use the strategies in more advanced and extensive ways.

In Chapter 2, a theory will be presented that has been developed from many, many classroom observations of teachers' work; from many, many discussions with teachers; from the literature on teaching for thinking; and from extensive feedback from students. Teaching strategies that are derived from the theory have been applied in classrooms at various educational levels, from the primary grades, through all the elementary grades, to the secondary schools, and on to universities and teacher workshops. Experimental studies have been conducted to gather data from student performance in achievement, in thinking, and in self-perceptions of learning and growth. In short, the theory being presented in Chapter 2 has a history, and it has, so far, not been found wanting.

So here is an invitation to teachers to examine the theory for themselves, to see if it "makes sense," and if it does, to begin to use some of the classroom activities and strategies to gather data from their own observations about the effectiveness of the theory. The most important test will be, of course, to see if the activities and the classroom strategies work in fulfilling the goals we all say we want for our students. Nothing less than that should be acceptable.

CHAPTER 2

Teaching for Thinking

A Curriculum Framework
for Classroom Practice

He shuffled into the room—all 5' 8" of him, sweaty and puffing from playing in the school yard, the kids making the most of those precious last few moments of the summer weather. He looked me right in the eye, and I saw a shy, sweet smile come to his lips. I returned his smile, and his eyes brightened. I thought of Joey, in my last year's class, who had written in his journal, "A good teacher must have love for all the children, even the bad ones." My worries about Bobby's advance billing from former teachers melted, and I promised myself that I'd find a way to work with him.

After a few days, the school records about his earlier behavior were borne out by my own observations. He seemed unable to function without close supervision and structuring, unable to stick to a job and finish it on his own without calling me over for help numerous times. He seemed unable to make choices, to think things out for himself. I saw too, his racially prejudiced outbursts, his extreme dogmatism in presenting his opinions as truths. As I put together the data I'd collected from his former teachers' anecdotal reports and my own observations, I found that he was entirely dependent on others to do his thinking for him. His dependency behaviors seemed acute, yet there were no indications of any physical problems or emotional ones.

As I studied his presenting behaviors and began to consider his instructional needs, the Raths thinking theory gave me the guidelines for my teaching plans.

A THINKING THEORY

Louis E. Raths (Raths, Wasserman, Jonas, & Rothstein, 1966) spent more than 1,000 hours working with classroom teachers observing children's behavior. His field research enabled him to generate a theory of thinking that has permitted teachers to understand the link between inadequate development of thinking abilities and student behavior. The theory suggests that certain behaviors, seen persistently and in the extreme, may be a sign that students have had insufficient opportunities to develop their higher-order mental skills. The theory also suggests that if teachers were to provide these students with extensive practice in certain higher-order mental tasks, these maladaptive behaviors would diminish over time and be replaced by more thoughtful ways of behaving (Raths, Wasserman, Jonas, & Rothstein, 1986).

Most teachers implicitly understand the relationship between thinking and behavior. For example, when a teacher presents a group of students with a problem such as, "How would you figure out how to weigh a giraffe?" that teacher will quickly be able to discern the quality and kind of thinking that goes into their responses by listening to and observing how they reply. For example, some students would immediately begin by suggesting several possible ways of figuring this out. Other students might not begin at all. Instead, they would ask: "I don't get it. What do you want us to do? I don't understand what you mean." Or even worse, "We didn't study giraffes yet."

As teachers observe these behaviors, they are likely to say that the students who come up with viable solutions have a greater capacity for imaginative and inventive thought. They are also likely to observe that the students who are unable to get started, who need more help, who "don't understand," are unable to use their cognitive skills in problem-solving situations. They see that these students need more help from the teacher and that given tasks that require higher-level thinking, they lack the cognitive resources to deal with them. When such dysfunctions persist, when they are seen over the long term, and in response to many tasks that require independent thought, and when factors of physical or emotional problems can be ruled out, the teacher might hypothesize that such students are lacking skill in their higher-order mental functioning (Raths et al., 1986).

Raths's theory identifies eight behavioral patterns that are considered indicators of deficits in higher-order mental functioning. Embedded in their descriptions is the nature of the inadequacy revealed as students respond to learning challenges:

- Extreme impulsiveness
- Overdependence on the teacher
- Inability to concentrate
- Missing the meaning
- Extreme dogmatism
- Inflexibility
- Lack of confidence in one's own thinking
- Unwillingness to think

And while we all may engage in such behaviors on occasion, in some students these behaviors occur in persistent, acute, and persevering forms. The theory suggests that when physical and emotional factors are ruled out as possible causes, the behaviors are likely to be evidence of students' underdeveloped habits of intelligent thinking.

One of the many positives about Raths's theory is that it has been built on the basis of teacher observations in classroom practice. It is clear and unambiguous. It enables teachers to identify certain maladaptive pupil behaviors and allows for the generation of hypotheses that can be easily tested by teachers. It equips teachers with some valuable tools to deal more effectively with these nonproductive behaviors. Moreover, as the theory has evolved over the years, it has contributed in substantive ways to professional discourse about thinking in educational practice (Raths et al., 1986; Wassermann, 1987).

Much research in the area of "thinking skills development" has been carried out in the past 40 years that lends support to Raths's theory that thinking skills, like other sets of skills, can be developed and learned. (See, e.g., Costa, 1985; Paul & Elder, 2002; Pogrow, 2005; Segal, Chipman, & Glaser, 1985; Sternberg, 1987.) What is important in designing curriculum tasks to develop such intelligent habits of mind is that we ensure a means-ends connect—that is, that the curriculum activities and teaching strategies we design and use are compatible with the goals of elevating more intelligent mental functioning. Not every teaching strategy and curriculum activity fills this goal.

Here, too, Raths's work is helpful for teachers. He offers 14 "thinking operations"—specific mental functions that serve as guidelines for developing classroom activities (Raths, et al., 1986). These operations include

- Comparing
- Interpreting data
- Observing
- Summarizing
- Classifying
- Making decisions
- Suggesting hypotheses
- Imagining and creating
- Criticizing and evaluating
- Designing projects and investigations
- Identifying assumptions
- Applying principles in new situations
- Gathering and organizing data
- Coding to become aware of certain patterns of thinking

A cursory examination of these mental operations reveals that each requires a student to "do something more" with information—something *more* than merely absorbing it from a page and recalling the facts. This "more" involves more sophisticated and intelligent examination of that information; the analysis leads to increased understanding of the important ideas.

While Pogrow (2005) and Paul and Elder (2002) have developed programs where "thinking" is a separate subject to be taught, Raths's position is that thinking should be an integral part of every curriculum area; that is, teaching subject matter with an emphasis on thinking.

CLASSROOM QUESTIONS AND THINKING THEORY

Since the publication of the first edition of *Teaching for Thinking: Theory and Application* (Raths, Wassermann, Jonas, & Rothstein, 1966), a great deal of research and development has occurred from which an additional dimension of the theory has evolved. While the thinking operations still serve as helpful guidelines to the generation of curriculum tasks, the nature of a teacher's questions and responses in conducting a classroom discussion that promotes thoughtful and intelligent examination of the "big ideas" in the curriculum has been found to be significant in furthering thinking skills development.

The early work of Parsons (1971) and Flanders (1970) was significant in raising awareness of the relationship between teachers' questions and student thinking. Their work led to the development of a question/response analysis tool (Wassermann, 2004) that provides teachers with a useful framework for analyzing their own questions and responses in teacher-student discussions. Chapters 3 and 4 deal with these questioning and responding strategies.

NEW DEVELOPMENTS IN APPLYING THINKING THEORY

In Chapter 1, I wrote that good theory should serve as a beacon for teachers to inform their classroom practices. In the years since the Raths theory was first published, much work has occurred in classrooms at all levels of instruction, with considerable benefit to student learning and thinking. These field trials have led to new insights and new understandings about the classroom applications of the theory. Although the theory has not changed, the applications have become more refined.

Originally, the thinking operations formed a basis for creating classroom activities within the context of the subject areas. (See, e.g., Raths, et al., 1986, Chapters 2 and 3). Teachers used existing curriculum content and created learning tasks using the 14 thinking operations as a basis for student inquiry into the content (for example, *comparing* the Declaration of Independence to the Magna Carta by looking for similarities and differences, making *observations* of the periodic table, *suggesting hypotheses* to identify possible reasons for the church's suppression of Galileo's theory of the solar system). It did not seem to matter in what order the thinking operations were used, nor was there any suggestion that there *should* be any hierarchy in incorporating the operations into the curriculum.

As the theory evolved, and as new research and new field trials were conducted, it was found that student learning and thinking are further enhanced when the operations are positioned in a particular framework (Wassermann, 2000; Wassermann & Ivany, 1996). The new framework reconfigures the operations and sets them in a progression, taking the learner from gathering data by making observations *(knowing)*, to analyzing information *(understanding)*, to applying what is known to problem solving *(knowing how)*. Thus, in learning new material, students would first begin with the gathering of data through their own *observations*. Observations might be made, for example, through the viewing of a film or a DVD, examining an article or reading a story, examining the data in a graph or in a table, observing the structure of a bridge, examining a list of metaphors, measuring the height of "bounce" of different-size balls, examining the voting record of a member of the U.S. Senate, examining "original" historical documents, studying the behavior of a pet, and so on. The examples of the ways in which students can gather knowledge through observing are numerous—and many, many curriculum experiences, in virtually every subject area, can be introduced through requesting that students make observations.

The second stage in the progression requires students to process the acquired information—by using the operations of comparing, classifying, coding for certain patterns of thinking, looking for assumptions, suggesting hypotheses, summarizing, and interpreting data. These operations call for different ways and different opportunities for students to deepen their understanding, by subjecting the information to different kinds of analyses. At this second stage, for example, students can compare two historical documents, two stories, two celebrity figures, two different ways of solving a math problem, two presidents, warm-blooded and cold-blooded animals, and so forth. They can classify historical documents, stories in a short story collection, lists of celebrity figures, different solutions to math problems, lists of animals, and more. They can look for assumptions in televised speeches, in newspaper editorials, in advertisements, in projections of the future, in conclusions made after a science experiment, and the like. They can suggest hypotheses to explain why some people need glasses, why some are allergic to different foods, why rents are more expensive in different parts of town, why ball players earn more money than teachers, what makes some people more popular than others, why some people are short and others are tall, or why the moon causes tides to rise and fall. These are only a very few examples of how data coming from observations can be analyzed. I call this data-processing stage building *understanding*. Students are aided in this process through the teacher's use of higher-order questioning.

In the third stage, students are given opportunities to apply what they know, to put what they know into practice. This step involves the operations of problem solving, applying principles to new situations, decision making, designing projects, imagining, and creating. Students can apply what they know in designing an investigation to determine how they can tell that the moon affects tides; how a telephone survey can be used to gather data about preferences; how a campaign might be mounted to deal with littering in the school yard; how a campaign might be mounted to support recycling efforts in the school; how money might be raised to support worthwhile causes; how elementary school students might have an effective voice in addressing world problems, such as child labor; or how a project might be designed to demonstrate how the respiratory system works in humans or in animals. In this *knowing how* stage, the teacher's use of selective higher-order questions once more plays a major role in enabling students' knowing how.

At a fourth stage, the teacher uses higher-order questions to help students reflect on their work. What was good about what they did? What would they like to have improved? Where does their work need "fixing"? What kind of fixing is needed? What new insights were acquired? What additional information is needed? And most important, what are the standards by which these assessments are being made? Reflection on a student's own learning experiences and making self-assessments revisits what has been learned, puts a student's work through his or her own critical eye, and opens the door for further inquiry. This stage uses the operation of criticizing and evaluating and puts students on the pathway of becoming critical evaluators and judges of their own work.

By reconfiguring the operations into this new framework (see Figure 2.1) and developing curriculum experiences around such a framework, teachers can take students through the learning stages of gathering information, making meaning of that information, and using that information in practical ways. The end result of this structuring is that students increase their knowledge base, deepen their understanding, and learn how to use that information in solving problems. Student learning and thinking are the beneficiaries of this approach and the boundaries of student intelligence are advanced.

It is my hope that this new operational framework for designing curriculum with an emphasis on higher-order thinking and teaching for understanding will enable teachers to build curriculum experiences to enrich students' knowledge, deepen understanding of the big ideas, help them to apply knowledge, and help them grow in the self evaluation of their work. Through these efforts, students will become empowered as thinkers, and their learning will have more meaning.

The first step in moving in the direction of a teaching-for-thinking classroom involves the examination of the kinds of questions and responses used in teacher-student discussions that promote quality of thought. That is the subject of Chapters 3 and 4 in Part II.

Figure 2.1. Teaching-for-Thinking Operations in a Curriculum Framework

---

Stage 1: Gathering knowledge through observing.

Stage 2: Promoting understanding through comparing, classifying, coding for certain patterns of thinking, looking for assumptions, suggesting hypotheses, summarizing, and interpreting data.

Stage 3: Applying knowledge through problem solving, designing projects and investigations, applying principles to new situations, making decisions, imagining and creating.

Stage 4: Reflecting on action through evaluating and assessing.

PART II

Teaching Strategies: Conducting Effective Classroom Discussions

CHAPTER 3

Keys to Productive Classroom Discussions

A group of 6th-grade students is observing a map of their community in Marin County, California. The objective of the activity is for students to take first steps in map study, particularly with respect to understanding that maps are graphic representations of places, and to apply intelligent reasoning to their observations. The big ideas behind this map study are the following:

- Maps are graphic representations of places
- Maps provide information about location, distance, scale and geographical orientation
- The information contained in maps has specific parameters

At first the students work in small, self-directed study groups, making observations on their own. This initial work is followed by whole-class discussion, directed by the teacher. The discussion begins with the teacher's questions calling for the students' observations (information gathering), which she follows up with questions calling for analysis (promoting understanding) of the information gathered:

Teacher: Tell me about some of the observations you made.
(Several children raise their hands.)
Teacher: You'd like to begin, Jonah?
Jonah: I see these blue lines, and I think they are the streets. You can see that there are the names of the streets inside those blue lines.
Teacher: The blue lines seem to you to be the streets, and there is some evidence to support that, since each blue line has a street name.
Jonah: Yeh. That's how I know they are streets, because of the way the lines are drawn and because they have street names.
Teacher: The way the lines are drawn also indicates that these are streets. Thank you, Jonah. Anyone else like to add an observation?
Bonnie: I agree with Jonah. I think they are the streets. And I know

there is a street named San Remo right downtown. And here, on the map, this blue line is marked San Remo.

Teacher: What you have observed, Bonnie, supports Jonah's idea and what's more, you know there is a street named San Remo downtown and that matches what you've seen in the map. So you can say that this map is showing the streets of our town.

Bonnie: Yeah.

Teacher: Thanks, Bonnie. Anyone else have an observation to add?

Meg: I think this map shows *all* the streets of Fairfax.

Teacher: You believe that all the streets are shown on the map.

Meg: Yeah.

Teacher: I'm wondering how you can tell that all the streets are included. Do you have any evidence to support that, Meg?

Meg: Well, I just think that a map would have all the streets. Otherwise, how would it be a good map?

Teacher: It makes sense to you that a good map should have all the streets in it. No streets should be left out. That is an assumption you are making, Meg?

Meg: Yeah, I'm assuming. But I think it's true.

Teacher: You like that assumption. Otherwise, you think the map wouldn't be very useful, if some of the streets were not included.

Meg: Yeah.

Teacher: I wonder how you could test that out. To figure out if that assumption is, in fact, true. Any thoughts on that, Meg?

Meg: I need to think about that.

Teacher: Sure. Let me know when you want me to come back to you. I'd like to hear some other observations, if you have them.

George: I can see where some of the downtown buildings are located. I can see the courthouse. (He points to it on the map. The other children look at the place where he is pointing.)

Teacher: You can locate the street where the courthouse is. What are some other observations you can make, George, about the location of the courthouse?

George: Well, I can see that it is on Center Street—you see, there's the name right there. And I just know that the courthouse is on Center Street.

Teacher: So what you have observed on the map is the same as what you have observed downtown about the courthouse.

George: Yeah.

Teacher: Thanks, George. Any other observations?

Roxie: I'm looking at the boundaries of the map. I'm looking at where the map ends, on all sides.

Teacher: What observations have you made about the boundaries, Roxie?

Roxie: Well, I can see that the map ends, here, at the top, at Avery Park. And on this side, it ends at the freeway. And down here, at the bottom, it ends at the lake. And here (points to the left side of the map), it just stops at some streets.

Teacher: You are observing the outer boundaries of the map, Roxie.

From that, you are able to tell the areas the map includes, and
where the map stops.
Roxie: Yeah. The boundaries of the map.
Teacher: Thanks, Roxie. Let's see. You've observed that this map
shows the streets and it also shows some important buildings
like the courthouse. Roxie has added that the map has specific
boundaries. Thank you all for those observations. Now, I wonder if
anyone can tell, from your observations, how you can get from place
to place. I mean, if you wanted to go from the courthouse to Avery
Park, how might the map help you to figure that out?

CONDITIONS THAT PROMOTE STUDENT THINKING

Teachers who have studied how classroom discussions contribute to foster-
ing students' intelligent habits of mind have identified what they consider
to be key conditions of productive discussions. These conditions include
the use of certain questions and responses that enable students to identify
what they know and to use their knowledge to understand the big ideas,
and they also include those conditions that create a climate that makes it
safe for them to think. Chapter 4 examines the ways in which a teacher's
questions and responses contribute to student thinking. This chapter deals
with those conditions that are central to building a climate of trust—one in
which students feel safe to offer their ideas. These essential conditions for
teaching-for-thinking discussions include

- Listening to, attending to, and apprehending students' statements
- Comprehending what students mean
- Waiting for students to formulate their ideas
- Being nonjudgmental in accepting students' responses
- Showing appreciation for students' ideas
- Focusing discussion on the examination of the issues, rather than on
  finding the "right" answers
- Being comfortable with lack of closure

Each of these conditions is discussed in the sections below. However, it is
important to keep in mind that at the other end of the interactive spectrum
are those conditions that also merit serious attention—those that crush students' chances to think. These are discussed later in the chapter.

Listening, Attending, Apprehending

On the surface, it seems a "no-brainer" to ask that teachers listen and attend to what students are saying. However, in the real life of the classroom,
with many pressures on teachers and many pulls on a teacher's attention, it

is less than easy to pay full attention to listen to, attend to, and apprehend a student's statement. Doing that requires the teacher to focus attention fully on the student, shutting out classroom noise. Eyes turned to the student, face full of interest, the teacher communicates with body language: "I am with you. I am listening to what you have to say." Listening is more than just hearing the words. It includes observing all behavioral cues as the words are being spoken; hearing nuance and voice inflection, observing particular words chosen to express certain ideas, and noticing where the statement is given emphasis. When all that occurs, the teacher is doing what Freire (1983) calls "apprehending"—taking in and making meaning of the totality.

Listening, attending, and apprehending require that the teacher's mind be freed, so it is open to hear and observe. One cannot listen and attend if one is, at the same moment, thinking of what Marvin is doing in the rear of the class. Nothing should get in the way of full concentration on the student and the student's statement.

The ability to do this provides the teacher with the information needed to formulate intelligent responses. It also creates the climate in which respect for students and for their ideas is palpable and makes it safe for students to offer their ideas. Even more, it contributes to the essential condition of interactive teaching—that is, the teacher and students are engaging in a dialogue in which all parties together are searching to understand, creating, in Christensen's (1995) words, "a community of learners." The teacher's skill in listening, attending, and apprehending is basic to the art of a teaching-for-thinking discussion, and it is on this foundation that all the other skills rest.

Comprehending What Students Mean

Not every student is articulate. Not every one is able to express his or her ideas clearly. Even good ideas may elude effective expression. If teachers are going to be able to respond productively—in a way that leads to greater understanding—it is important that a student's idea is clearly understood.

Listening, attending, and apprehending skills are the first steps in comprehending a student's meaning. If this effort does not lead to understanding, it is fair game to ask for clarification; for example:

- I'm not sure I understand you. Can you help me?
- Let's see if I've understood you correctly. I'll try to say it back to you, and then you can tell me if I've got it right.
- Help me to understand. Can you say that in a different way?

When asking for clarification, the teacher assumes the burden of not comprehending. The student is not penalized or made to feel stupid for not stating his or her ideas clearly. The objective is for the student to tell it as he or she wants it told, and for the teacher to grasp the meaning. This comprehension provides a second step in enabling the teacher to formulate an appropriate response.

Waiting for Students to Formulate Their Ideas

Teachers are more often than not in a race with the clock, trying to get all that needs to be done completed by the end of the day. While I know that pressure intimately and have had nightmares about students leaving class in June with still so much more I wanted to teach undone, nevertheless, I have the temerity to suggest that if teaching for thinking is to occur, teachers must put aside the rush to finish, and allow students time to think. Thinking takes time. Good ideas take time to formulate, to "hatch." Unfortunately, we cannot have it both ways. We cannot have a classroom in which thinking is to flourish, as well be in a rush to finish. Thinking must trump "covering all of the lesson." And while it may seem heresy to suggest this, I also suggest that teachers need to decide which is the more important and urgent goal.

Teachers who are new to "wait time" have invented strategies that help them to remember to take their time, to hold off until the student has had a chance to offer his or her ideas. Any strategy that is effective can be used. The key is to learn to wait, and wait, so that pupils have time to think, to formulate their ideas.

Being Nonjudgmental in Accepting Students' Responses; Appreciating Students' Ideas

Making it safe for students to express their ideas is at the heart of productive teacher-student discussions. When students are fearful that their ideas are going to be judged as right or wrong, they are less likely to volunteer them. If ideas are going to be penalized, few students will risk offering them. If ideas are going to be rewarded, only those who are certain that they have the "correct" ideas will volunteer them.

Judgments fall easily from teachers' lips—and some of us think that that is a big part of the teacher's job: to tell the kids when they are right and when they are wrong. However, these judgments are anathema to a climate in which thinking new and original ideas may flourish. This may be one of the most difficult principles of a teaching-for-thinking interactive dialogue—for teachers to say, "I see," rather than, "That's good," or even, "That's an interesting idea." Avoiding judgments does not preclude showing appreciation for a student's contribution. So, saying, "Thanks, Megan, for contributing your ideas," is not only acceptable, but a welcome input to the discussions. The caveat in showing appreciation is the teacher's genuineness in offering it. Anything that sounds phony is counterproductive.

Focusing Discussion on Examining Issues Instead of Finding the Answers; Being Comfortable with Lack of Closure

I have linked these two principles together, since they are two pieces of a greater whole. The teacher's ability to dwell in the land of uncertainty—in which the emphasis in the discussion is on examination, rather than on finding the only acceptable answer—is directly connected to that teacher's comfort with lack of closure. The ability to do this requires, at heart, a teacher's belief that this more open-ended discussion is of benefit to students.

The need for certainty, for the security that closure brings, seems to be a built-in feature of our human makeup. The human organism needs to resolve ambiguity. When closure can be reached, it is accompanied by a palpable sigh of relief—a sort of psychological "whew." Having answers gives security. Not knowing for certain; having to weigh alternatives, to examine assumptions, to suspend judgment; trying to understand what is going on; making informed judgments; and risking options provokes anxiety. I don't deny it; it feels good to know the answers. It feels affirming when students can tell you, with certainty, that Winnipeg is the capital of Manitoba and that it was Paul Revere who designed the state seal of Massachusetts. It is more stressful to have to take the risks involved in applying knowledge to figure out potential solutions to problems, where answers are rarely clear, where the meaning we make is our own, and where the best answer is often, "It depends." Even experienced teachers who acknowledge ambiguity and operate with a higher tolerance for it often wish for the relief that a clear, definitive answer can bring. This is especially true for beginning teachers, who suffer from insecurities associated with their lack of experience and for whom "good" answers appear to reduce the stresses of teaching. We look to our teachers, to workshops, and to books to tell us with certainty what is *right*. But in the end, as most teachers know, we are usually left to our own resources.

However, it is not the "definitive answer" that allows a student to progress from knowing to understanding and then to problem solving. For to know definitive answers does not an educated person make, because knowledge alone is far from a guarantee that a person will behave intelligently, wisely, or competently.

Classroom discussions in which the teacher can approach a student's response and say, "Tell me more," or, perhaps, "I'm wondering how you figured that out," or, "Perhaps you have some data to support your idea," are all invitations for students to examine further. These questions/responses do not lead to answers; they call for further inquiry. They insist on clarity of thinking, upon reflection about a position, upon examples and data to support an idea. The teacher's responses call for students' intelligent examination that leads to increased understanding and potential for action. Such questions and responses take students much further in their conceptualizations than a definitive answer would do. They keep the lines of inquiry open.

The absence of closure may, at first, be somewhat disconcerting. Yet after time, many teachers find that relinquishing the need for certainty is wonderfully liberating.

CONDITIONS THAT LIMIT AND ACTUALLY CRUSH STUDENT THINKING

Just as there are certain key elements of classroom discussions that enable student thinking, there are certain elements in teachers' questions and responses that crush thinking. As much as we might not like to believe it, such teacher responses create major obstacles for students to think their own thoughts, examine ideas, and venture theories that are innovative and that go beyond what is expected. And regrettably, when such stifling of student thinking is the pattern of teacher-student interactions over the long term, students' intelligent habits of mind wither and atrophy from lack of use.

The teacher who agrees or disagrees with a student's statement, perhaps without meaning to, puts a finish on students' thinking; there is no requirement that they think further. When teachers rush a discussion and don't give students chances to think, this denies the opportunity to exercise intelligent habits of mind. ("No matter what I do in the Civil War unit, Grant has to be in Richmond by Thanksgiving!")

When the teacher tells the students what he or she thinks, this too denies students the chance to think things through for themselves. When the teacher talks too much, explains things his or her way, gives information, or tells students what to think, these seemingly innocuous responses seriously delimit opportunities for students to exercise their own brain power. When the teacher cuts a student off, heckles or puts down a student's idea, responds with sarcasm, or otherwise belittles a student's response, students become fearful of thinking and therefore suppress their motivation to think for themselves.

CAVEATS

Long-term classroom experiences with "discussion teaching" have provided an abundance of evidence to show that when positive interactive conditions are in play, a teaching-for-thinking discussion is unsurpassed in its ability to transform students from "lesson learners" into thoughtful, considerate, productive learners. Teachers who have engaged students in these ways have almost immediately seen positive results in their classrooms.

But make no mistake—just as there is no free lunch, discussion teaching has its caveats. There is a powerful force at play when teachers begin by asking students questions, rather than setting themselves up as the purveyors of "truth." Students who experience the growing sense of personal power that such discussions bring, are less likely to be blindly obedient, submissive, and complaisant. Furthermore, if the teacher is insensitive and uses questions to interrogate, forgetting that a student has feelings, this can be damaging to the student's sense of self, putting that student on the defensive, unwilling to take the risk of responding further.

Before bringing this chapter to a close, I will remind teachers that the key elements used in a teaching-for-thinking discussion are not in evidence every single moment of every teaching day. There are times when a teacher will want to tell students what he or she thinks ("I think that what happened on the playground this recess was not representative of thoughtful behavior on the part of some students"). There are times when a teacher wants to make a judgment ("Mona, that story you wrote was so touching, it brought tears to my eyes"). There are times when a teacher will want students to know definitive answers ("So how much is 9 times 6?"). And there are times when the teacher will agree or disagree with a student, give information, and explain certain procedures. In other words, there is a time for productive classroom discussions, in which the objective is to elevate students' intelligent habits of mind, and there are times for other kinds of responses. The art of a teaching-for-thinking discussion, and in fact, the art of teaching, is for the teacher to know what the goals are and then use those teaching strategies that are the best for attaining those goals—so that what we do is entirely congruent with what we hope to accomplish: consistently connecting our means with our ends.

CHAPTER 4

Asking the Right Questions

Television journalism has, with a few notable exceptions, fallen into serious disrepute. There are likely many factors contributing to this state of affairs, but none so telling as the way in which TV reporters are seen to obtain information from interviewees. For example, during the earliest days of the Gulf war, while an anxious world sat glued to the TV, sponging up every factoid that might relieve some of their anxiety, reporters tried to hold viewer attention by hastily arranged interviews to fill up airtime, resulting in theater of the absurd. On one occasion, when SCUD missiles fell in residential neighborhoods in Tel Aviv, reporters were heard to ask frightened and disoriented citizens, "So how did you feel when the SCUD missile landed?" Such a question is what Carkhuff (1969) calls a "stupid question"—insensitive, disrespectful, and thoughtless. Such questions trivialize what is emotionally or intellectually complex.

If you've ever been asked a stupid question, you will immediately understand Carkhuff's classification. Stupid questions are insulting. They evoke anger and frustration. However, if the questioner happens to be a person of authority, such as a television reporter, the victim might feign politeness and scramble mentally for something to say; "Oh, we were scared," some did reply in the TV interviews in Tel Aviv.

We learn nothing from that response that we had not known before. Of course people are scared when bombs fall in their neighborhood. What do we expect? Suddenly the question becomes more than stupid. It reduces to banality what is terrifying and horrifying. TV news interviews are not the only place where stupid questions are heard. However, the example serves as an appropriate opener to the discussion of the art of the question.

From this single example, it is evident that questions may fall into categories other than the "higher order" and "lower order" classifications commonly associated with teaching for thinking (e.g., Bloom, 1956). It is also possible to see that questions have the potential to provoke powerful emotional responses, which are likely to affect substantially the subsequent response of a student. To look beyond higher order and lower order; to understand the power of questions to promote thoughtful examination; to know the differences between questions that are helpful and those that intimidate; to recognize the emotional burden that most questions carry; to use questions more wisely in enabling students to go from data gathering, to understanding, to application of understanding to practice, is at the heart of this chapter.

There is much more to a productive classroom discussion than merely making interrogative demands. If classroom discussions are to promote thoughtful examination of issues, then questioning and responding must be sensitive to many aspects of the interactive process. These include not only awareness of the construction of questions that call for students' examination of issues, but also how certain questions may provoke anxiety, thereby influencing the nature of the students' responses. A productive discussion that leads to examination of issues is not an interrogation. There is an interactive rhythm that consists of questions, interwoven with responses that lead to continued examination and exploration, in a climate that makes it safe for students to venture their ideas.

Good questions are clear in what they ask students to think about; they are not so broad or abstract that they defeat the process of thinking. Good questions invite; they do not command students to respond. Framing good questions requires a teacher to understand the purpose behind the question; that is, does the teacher want to know *what* the students know or *how* students use what they know to understand? Different purposes require different questions.

The art of questioning not only requires that teachers weave all these threads into an interactive dialogue, but also demands that teachers attend carefully to a student's response in order to formulate appropriate follow-up responses or questions that allow for continued inquiry. The conditions that create a climate for thinking identified in Chapter 3 set the stage for productive classroom discussions. This chapter focuses on types of questions, how they are constructed, and their potential effects on student thinking.

UNPRODUCTIVE QUESTIONS

There are several categories of unproductive questions that do little or nothing to promote meaningful examination of ideas. In some of the worst instances, they are intended to hurt and humiliate. Others dismiss students' ideas, implicitly suggesting that they have no value. Unproductive questions include stupid questions, questions that are too complex, questions that teachers themselves answer, trick questions, and questions that humiliate.

Stupid Questions

There are three ways to identify stupid questions: (1) the question does not attend to the student's idea, (2) the question is insensitive to the feelings or ideas being expressed, or (3) the question is irrelevant or disrespectful. For example:

> *Student:* My grandmother is very sick, and they think she's going to die.
> *Teacher:* How old is she?

> *Student:* I want to study dinosaurs.
> *Teacher:* Have you got a library card?

> *Student:* They tried to save the birds, but they couldn't. They were covered with the oil from the tanker ship.
> *Teacher:* So how can we stop pollution?

Questions That Are Too Complex

A second group of unproductive questions are those whose complexity lies beyond a student's ability to respond thoughtfully. These "too complex" questions are too broad in their scope and, consequently, they defeat intelligent examination. It is difficult to make an intelligent, succinct response to the question "What were the causes of World War I?"

An unintended consequence of such questions is that they are framed by teachers and heard by students as calls for a single, brief, unambiguous answer. Through such questions and answers, students learn that there are simple answers for exceedingly complex questions; and students learn to be satisfied with such simplicity, even as adults. Some examples of questions that are too broad in scope are

- Why is there pollution?
- Why did the early settlers in the United States want their independence from England?
- Why is the United States so dependent on oil from the Middle East?
- Why are people prejudiced?

Questions That Teachers Themselves Answer

Questions that teachers ask and then answer for themselves before students have a chance to respond are also unproductive. It is not that the questions are not good; they are unproductive because no student is given the chance to think about an intelligent response. Many teachers use these liberally in their discussions. Perhaps their intention is to get the students to think. But students have learned that if they do not respond within a few seconds, the teacher will answer his or her own question. There is no need for students to think; the teacher does it for them. There is no need for students even to listen. The teacher is carrying on a monologue. Some examples are

- So how come the Indians grew corn? (Pause). No one? Well, it's because the land was particularly suited to growing corn.
- How do we classify frogs? (Pause) Amphibians, right?
- What were some of the reasons for the westward movement? (Pause) OK. I'll give you a clue. Land, right? There was all that land out there, and people were beginning to feel the need for more space.

Trick Questions

Trick questions are deliberately (and sometimes maliciously) constructed to stump students. They are intended not only to show students up as pathetically inept, but also to show off the teacher's "smarts." When students cannot answer trick questions, the teacher waits and waits. Sometimes during this waiting period, the teacher will interject a derogatory comment to point up students' stupidity, for example: "I'm surprised at you for not knowing that." When the teacher finally gives the answer, he or she does so in such a cocky and arrogant way, both in tone and in body gesture, that all are convinced: The teacher is the brilliant one, and the students the great unwashed masses.

While trick questions may serve momentarily to bolster a teacher's ego, the price is heavy. These teachers gain neither student respect nor admiration. In fact, students see these teachers as small persons who are trying to make themselves large at students' expense.

Questions That Humiliate

In this category are questions laced with sarcasm, with inappropriate humor, with overt rejection, and with negative judgment about the student's response. It is hard to believe that teachers would deliberately set out to humiliate and degrade students. To give them the benefit of the doubt, perhaps these are misguided attempts to get students to "pull up their socks" and do good work. Yet, however well intentioned, questions that are full of sarcasm and rejection are so wounding, so utterly destructive, that students who experience them carry scars long after. How else would graduate students at a university learn to preface their questions with the self-protective introduction: "This may be a stupid question, but . . ."

Even to read them from a printed page is to wince; yet these questions have been heard from teachers:

- How come you don't know that? Is your memory that short?
- It's green? You think it's green? How on earth did you come up with that idea?
- Come on now, even you can answer this one, can't you?
- This is so easy, a 6-year-old could do it. How come you can't?

The effect of these questions is a diminishing of confidence, which for some students is the final crushing blow from which they may never be able to recover. For some students, it means never again speaking out in class, if they can help it.

LESS-THAN-PRODUCTIVE QUESTIONS

Some questions may call for students to examine ideas, but the way they are worded defeats productive examination. Some of these questions fall short because they deal with trivia instead of important issues. Some are too difficult for the students. In other examples, their wording is ambiguous. With a shift of phrase or focus, less-than-productive questions can become more productive.

Irrelevant Questions

Irrelevant questions do not require students to examine issues of substance. Often, these questions are tangential to the important issues in the lesson. The following examples of irrelevant questions come from a kindergarten classroom discussion on which animals would make good pets:

> *Cameron:* A parrot would make a good pet because it has a big tongue and it can talk.
> *Teacher:* How did you find out the parrot had a tongue?

> *Brian:* Elephants would make good pets because they could stomp on robbers if robbers came to your house.
> *Teacher:* What else could elephants do?

Put differently, these questions might zero in on the important issues in the lesson about pets. For example:

> I wonder, Cameron, do you suppose there is something about the parrot's tongue that makes it possible for it to talk?

> Brian, you think that elephants would make good pets. I wonder if you know anyone who has an elephant for a pet? How come, do you suppose?

Questions That Are Too Abstract

Questions that are too abstract defeat thoughtful examination largely because they reach beyond students' levels of experience and thus beyond what they are able to comprehend. These questions may appear to be challenging, but usually result in inappropriate answers, or worse, no answers.

To ask a 6-year-old, "How does a cell phone work without a plug-in?" is an example of asking a question that is too abstract and beyond a normal 6-year-old's conceptual grasp. Other highly abstract questions include such humdingers as

- Why do people litter?
- How do birds learn to fly?
- How do magnets get their power?

These questions are, of course, answerable in some fashion by even the inexperienced student. However, if the teacher's purpose is to promote student understanding of the big ideas, questions worded in the following ways are likely to yield more thoughtful, intelligent examination:

- What can you tell me about how all the candy wrappers and orange peels end up in the school yard? Do you have any hypotheses about it?
- How do you suppose birds learn to fly? Do you have any theories to explain it?
- You have observed how magnets have the power to attract and repel. Tell us about some of your observations.

When more challenging questions are phrased as requests for hypotheses, this brings them down to lower levels of abstraction. In that way, students may respond from observations rooted in their data gathering, thus building their habits of thinking and giving way to more intelligent discourse.

Questions That Are Too Ambiguous

Questions may be ambiguous because they are badly worded, thus confusing the student. Ambiguous questions may occur because the teacher lacks practice in formulating precisely worded questions; they may also occur when the teacher feels under stress. When the language of the question is unclear, or when the intent of the question is incomprehensible, student responses may be understandably inept. For example:

- What kinds of things did you come up with that you felt were going to be important for constructing your paper airplane?
- What was the extent and duration of the Dust Bowl drought?

Framing questions clearly and unambiguously first requires thinking about the question before stating it aloud. While such a strategy may take a moment or two of the teacher's time, that extra moment may be a good investment if it yields much better student responses.

Hit-and-Run Questions

Hit-and-run questions are part of some teachers' styles, the objective being to keep the discussion moving. Here, speed in question and answer takes precedence over the thoughtful examination of issues. Questions come in a rapid-fire assault and flit from issue to issue, without allowing for connections to be made and without allowing for productive examination of any single issue.

Here is an example of a hit-and-run question sequence from a 3rd-grade science lesson:

> *Teacher:* What kind of water is in the ocean?
> *Ken:* Salt.
> *Teacher:* Salt water. Right. Now how do we get freshwater?
> *Allison:* We could get it from the rain.
> *Teacher:* OK. So the rain is going to be freshwater. But how would we get the rainwater?
> *Marty:* Clouds.
> *Teacher:* But it would just fall to the ground. How would you get some?
> *Fiona:* In a cup.
> *Teacher:* OK. We could have a cup or bowl. Is there any other way of getting freshwater?
> *Jason:* Take some salt water and put it on a stove and boil it.
> *Teacher:* When we boil it, it's going to be freshwater?
> *Jason:* Yeah.
> *Teacher:* Nicole disagrees with you.
> *Nicole:* I tried that once, but it still tasted salty.

Teachers who recognize a hit-and-run pattern in their interactive dialogue may wish to consider some of the ideas in the section below in order to help shift their questioning and responding strategies away from the superficial toward examinations that lead to increased student understanding.

THE ART OF DISCUSSION TEACHING

The teacher's use of effective questions is basic to a good classroom discussion. These questions develop the habits of mind for students to think more intelligently about issues of consequence. The questions also bring a dynamic quality to class discussion, charging it with a positive energy that not only illuminates understanding, but also enlivens the entire class.

The road to using more productive questions in class discussions is not always a smooth one. Teachers who begin to use these questions may at first meet student resistance. Students who have been programmed to respond with single, correct answers may initially balk at having to develop their own ideas, to use their minds in more challenging ways. For students who have lived their school lives in the black-and-white world of certainty, questions that elevate ambiguity and uncertainty may at first create higher levels of dissonance and anxiety.

Yet the long-term payoff for using more productive questions that elevate dissonance is rich. Effectively used, they build habits of thinking. They give students practice in reasoning from the data, in arguing a point of view, in examining issues from more than one perspective, and in differentiating between fact and opinion. Dissonance is the key factor that keeps the channels of inquiry open, that keeps students thinking. If these learning goals are important to teachers, they will doubtless find creative and skillful ways to help students bridge the gap from initial resistance to more productive discourse. Experience with the process tells us that once students have crossed that bridge, once they have tasted the freedom of thinking for themselves, there is no going back.

An important strategy for effective discussion teaching is for teachers to identify, in advance, the big ideas to be examined in the lesson. With the big ideas explicitly articulated, it is possible for teachers to prepare themselves with a few questions to keep the discussion focused on the big ideas. This is so obvious that it may appear silly. Yet "teaching for the big ideas" is far from common practice in classrooms.

The big ideas underlying a discussion come from the teacher's sense of what is important. What, in the curriculum, warrants students' in-depth examination? What issues are worth knowing and understanding? When big ideas are vague or unarticulated, the likelihood is great that the follow up discussion becomes rambling, unfocused, and unproductive. (See Chapters 6–9, where examples of big ideas underlying each curriculum activity are offered.)

Characteristics of Productive Questions

There are some questions that make a mind buzz, some that are so provocative that they dwell in the mind for hours after they have been asked. These questions keep us thinking, searching for understanding. They are questions of magnitude, provoking examination of ideas worth knowing and thinking about. They are particularly nettlesome because responses to them are rarely rooted in certainty. It is the very reason they make us think.

If such questions cause so much cognitive dissonance, why are they classified as productive? The two dimensions—dissonance and productivity—are not, as one might expect, at odds. Productivity is born out of dissonance; the creation of something new emerges from mental labor. We cannot give birth to an idea, create, or invent without putting the mind through labor.

Responses to productive questions insist on the generation of something new. Whether the mind uses data to make analyses, as in comparing, classifying, or interpreting, or whether it is called on to leap from the data into brand-new thought, as in suggesting hypotheses, creating or evaluating, the mind is being challenged to bring forth new meanings, new configurations, new ideas. Because this is done in the absence of an absolute standard of right and wrong, such thoughts are left to dance in the great uncharted territory of uncertainty. But nothing new can ever emerge from the certainty of what is already known.

Nothing new or of consequence occurs when students are asked the question, "Who painted the *Mona Lisa*?" But consider what may be uncovered if the question is put more productively: "As you observe this painting, what, in your view, contributes to its ranking as a classical work of art?"

Nothing new or of consequence is examined through the question, "What group of people landed at Plymouth Rock?" But consider what may be examined, instead, with questions that take the learner down a more productive pathway: "What do you suppose were some of the very first experiences the Pilgrims had when they landed at Plymouth Rock in 1619? What data are you using to support your ideas?"

As in most matters of the curriculum, it is the teacher's choice that dictates the kinds of questions put to students. And teachers will invariably make choices that emphasize certain aspects of the curriculum, depending on their own values, educational beliefs, and issues they consider to be of significance. If teachers' needs for security are paramount, no amount of persuasion is likely to dissuade them from choosing questions that have clear and predetermined answers. Needs are never trumped by logical argument, nor are they negotiable. If teachers believe or may be persuaded to believe in the value of generative thinking, and if their needs do not constrain them from teaching in that muddy swampland of cognitive dissonance, it is likely that such teachers will choose the route of more productive questions.

Guidelines for Productive Questions

The guidelines below are offered for teachers who want to develop their skills as discussion teachers.

Questions that call for students to gather data and to think more generatively about issues of substance are drawn from the higher-order mental operations. These include questions calling for observing (gathering data), comparing, classifying, hypothesizing, evaluating, interpreting data, deciding, creating, and applying principles to new situations (Bloom, 1956; Raths et al., 1986). These higher-order operations may be explicitly contained in the questions. For example:

- What observations have you made about the way Matisse uses shapes in his paintings?
- How would you compare the American Revolution to the Civil War? What are some important differences? What are some similarities?

- What hypotheses can you suggest to explain the noise when a balloon bursts?

On the other hand, the operations may not be explicitly stated, but, instead, may be implied in the question. For example:

- What is your understanding of the events that led to the Great Depression of the 1930s? (interpreting data)
- How does the geography of the Andes bear on the climate, living conditions, culture, politics, and economics of South America? (hypothesizing)
- Which character in the story would you choose for a friend? (evaluating, deciding)

Questions that are clearly worded make it easier for the students to understand what is being asked of them and enable them to respond more intelligently. A teacher's conscious effort is required in constructing a clearly worded question—not easy to do "on one's feet." When teachers think that students are answering questions that are different from what the teacher thought he or she was asking, it may be helpful to reexamine how the question was constructed. The more teachers are conscious of the clarity demanded of questions, and the more they work on developing this skill, the easier it gets. A key to formulating clearly worded questions is the teacher's clarity about what is to be examined in the question. In focusing the question, it is helpful to ask: What is it that I want the students to think about? On what issue do I want to focus this question? This focusing requires teachers to make choices about those issues they believe worthy of examination. Here is an example of how this would work. The students in a social studies class have observed the following chart on world demographics in their textbook:

Global Village Demographics

If the world had a population of 1,000:
60 would control half the income.
500 would be hungry.
600 would live in shantytowns.
700 would be illiterate.

If the teacher chooses to focus on the big idea of unequal distribution of world resources, he or she might word the questions as follows:

- What observations can be made about how wealth is distributed in the Global Village?
- What, in your view, do these data mean in terms of world health and quality of life?
- How do you explain the skewing of the distribution of wealth? What hypotheses can you suggest that might explain it?

Using the same chart, another teacher might choose to focus on the big idea of control by the minority over the majority. Questions that would call for such examination might be worded as follows:

- What observations can be made from the data about the group with power and control?
- Where, in your view, does their power come from?
- What are some implications of these data for world economics? standard of living? world politics?

Questions that invite and are respectful of students' feelings and opinions create a climate of trust, in which they feel safe to offer their own ideas. Tone of voice, nuance of expression, the communication of a mutual searching for meaning, and the words that are used all contribute to the feel of the question. In attempting to frame questions as invitations, it is helpful to ask oneself: Am I inviting this student to join me in the examination of this issue?

If the question is offered as an invitation to join in exploration, students are likely to feel a lot safer in generating ideas. If the question contains a hidden hook on which the student is going to be impaled, if it seems threatening or hostile, or if it seems to be disrespectful, the students' anxiety level may thwart an intelligent response. If a teacher has a specific answer in mind for the question, revealed by tone of voice, then this will alert students that it is unsafe for them to respond with their own ideas, that they are safe only if they come up with the idea that the teacher is seeking.

The tone of a question reveals a teacher's underlying attitude toward students. If a teacher is respectful of students, sees them as partners in inquiry, and is comfortable in a nonjudgmental role, students will respond to questions as invitations to examine issues. On the other hand, if a teacher has an attitude that speaks clearly to who is in control and who has all the answers, then the teacher's questions are likely to reveal this, and students will not risk offering their own views.

In examining the issue of respect for students, teachers may ask themselves: Am I inviting students to examine ideas in a forum of true inquiry? Am I able to free myself from an authority role when responding to students' ideas and opinions? Am I able to avoid making positive or negative judgments about the responses given?

Questions that are productive make a demand on students to think about important issues. Thoughtful reflection makes cognitive demands different from those of coming up with "correct" answers. It requires the consideration of the issue, the examination of data, the consideration of alternatives, and the offering of examples—in short, the suspension of judgment and the elevation of ambiguity. Student thinking about issues is provoked when questions call for comparisons to be made, for observations, for setting up classifications, for evaluating and judging, for making choices, for interpreting data, for generating hypotheses, and for applying principles to new situations.

Some examples of questions that call for thoughtful reflection include:

- What, in your view, explains the appeal of celebrities?
- What do you see as some advantages of the parliamentary system of government? What arguments would you use to support a parliamentary system in the United States?
- What do you know about the Panama Canal? What, in your view, were some significant issues related to the building of the canal?

Compare the kind of thinking these questions demand with "Name 3 celebrities" or "Name the kind of system of government in the United States" or "In what year was the Panama Canal built?"

Questions that require students to show how they reason from the data allow them to use what they know in order to understand important concepts. Questions that merely determine what students can recall will neither enliven discussion nor allow for the examination of ideas. While it is certainly valuable to know certain pieces of information, these pieces become useful only when we can put them together to understand what is important. Putting them to work means being able to jiggle them around cognitively, to sort and process them, so that meanings are revealed. Productive questions enable students to shed light on meanings and increase understanding.

In asking productive questions, teachers do not abandon their charge to inform students and build their knowledge base. However, they put the emphasis on using knowledge to increase understanding. So instead of asking, "Who are the chief characters in *Macbeth*?" teachers ask: "What roles do the characters in *Macbeth* play? How, in your view, do the characters' interactions with each other contribute to the tension in the play?"

"Why" questions, which are generally very challenging, can be softened by narrowing their focus. When teachers strive to use more productive questions, there is a great tendency to fall back on "why" questions. "Why?" or "Why do you think so?" come easily to the lips and they, of course, challenge students to think. However, there is a downside to "why" questions. For no matter how careful the tone, "why" sounds inquisitorial. Students feel they are being put on the spot. "Why do you think so?" causes students to feel defensive. And feeling defensive is not conducive to thinking. It is more productive to reframe "why" questions in some of these ways:

- Tell me a little more about what you mean.
- You may have some data to support that position.

- Can you perhaps give some examples?
- I'm wondering how you figured that out. Can you help me understand?

Tough questions are made "softer" by turning them into declarative statements. It is less threatening to students to hear questions phrased in a gentler, less aggressive form. When questions can be softer in tone, students do not have to wade through layers of initial anxiety before offering their ideas. For example, instead of asking, "What examples can you give?" the teacher might say, "You may have some examples to support your statements." Another way of reducing the aggressive tone of a question is to frame it in less confrontational language. For example, instead of asking, "Is there an inconsistency between those two statements you have just made?" the teacher may say, "Help me to understand. I'm seeing an inconsistency in your two statements. Have I misunderstood you?"

These are differences not so much in substance as in tone. Some teachers may prefer a more aggressive questioning mode; others will opt for the softer, less forceful way. In determining your mode, ask yourself, With this particular group of students, what questioning tone is likely to get the better result?

Letting Go of the Evaluative Response

One of the necessary adjuncts of productive discussions is the teacher's ability to resist the tendency to evaluate every student response. Teachers have become habituated to using evaluative utterances quite automatically: "Good idea, Fiona." "That's interesting, Lloyd." "Not quite on the mark, Justin." Although some claim that students need evaluative encouragement to stimulate further participation, such responses are more likely to cut off further discussion than facilitate it. Try letting go of evaluative responses for one class discussion and then ask students for their perceptions of the experience. While initially students who have become accustomed to hearing "Good" and may feel unsettled when judgments are not forthcoming, over time, they will much prefer it. Letting go of evaluative responses does not mean being unappreciative of students' ideas. But there is a considerable difference in impact between "Good answer, Fiona," and "Thanks for sharing your thinking on that issue, Fiona."

THE WELL-ORCHESTRATED DISCUSSION

It is obvious that the well-balanced, productive discussion is not made up entirely of a string of questions, no matter how well each meets the various criteria for provoking thought. The framing of productive questions is only one measure of good discussion teaching. The other lies in the teacher's ability to listen, to attend to what the student is saying, and to intersperse productive questions with other responses that require students to reexamine their ideas. A discussion that consists only of questions will drive the discourse upward and outward too rapidly, without allowing students a chance to think in and around the big ideas. New questions invariably shift the discussion to new issues. Before doing this, teachers will wish also to use responses that dig more deeply, before shifting gears into new territory.

Here is an example of how this might work in a Grade 4 discussion on the Zuni Indians:

> *Teacher:* Tell me what observations you made about the ways of life of
>   the Zuni.
> *Tamar:* Well, they were primarily agricultural.

If the teacher chooses a question at this point—for example, "What other observations have you made about them?"—this question immediately shifts the discourse away from the reexamination of the student's idea that the Zuni's way of life is agricultural, to other aspects of their way of life. To require the student to reach for deeper meanings, the teacher might respond with

> Tell me more about how being agricultural marked their lives. (Asks for
> more information—for the student to elaborate on what is meant by
> "agricultural.")

By responding directly to the student's statement, the teacher calls for a reexamination of the idea presented. This is done for several reasons. First, such a response communicates that the teacher has heard the student's idea. Second, when the idea is "played back" for the student to reexamine, the student takes responsibility for it. Such attention to students' ideas creates habits of thinking. Students must think before they speak. They learn that what they say will be subject to critical self-scrutiny. Moreover, it requires that the student go beyond that response to dig into the meaning of what it meant to be agricultural. The search for more understanding is abetted by such responses.

> *Tamar:* I think it means that they grew all their own stuff. Like their food
>   and stuff.
> *Teacher:* (Options for responding)
>   * They grew their own food. (Paraphrases)
>   * What did they do for those things they were not able to grow?
>   (Challenges; asks student to go beyond the idea of being
>   agricultural and examine other ways in which the Zuni obtained
>   other necessities of life.)
>   * What did they grow? (Asks for specific information; asks for
>   answers)
>   * So they did a lot of farming. (Interprets the student's statement.)

As the teacher-student dialogue evolves, the teacher listens and apprehends and has a variety of options with respect to a subsequent response. Choosing a paraphrase would allows for deeper examination of what it means to depend on farming for food; the challenge question would shift the discourse into another realm, and away from the further examination of an agricultural culture; the information question redirects the inquiry toward a discussion of the types of food grown and limits the inquiry to specifics. The interpreting response examines "agricultural" from the type of work that involved. The teacher chooses to "interpret," to continue the examination of what it means to be an agricultural society from the vantage point of the work involved. The student responds:

> *Tamar:* Yeah. They had to do a lot of farming to grow their own stuff. But I think it was the women who did the farming but the men went out to hunt.
> *Teacher:* (Options for responding)
> - The women were the farmers. They were the ones who grew the food. (Paraphrases)
> - So some of the food was grown, but the men hunted for other kinds of food. (Paraphrases and interprets what the men hunted)
> - Why do you suppose that men needed to hunt for other kinds of food? (Challenges; asks for hypotheses)

If the teacher chooses to paraphrase, she will keep the inquiry focused on the food growing and the role of the women in an agricultural society; if she chooses to paraphrase and interpret what the men hunted, she opens up the possibility for the dialogue to shift to the kind of food not grown; if she raises the challenging question of asking why hunting was needed to supplement what was grown, the discourse shifts into new territory. The choice the teacher makes will, of course, direct the pathway of the inquiry. The teacher chooses to paraphrase and interpret, and Tamar responds:

> Tamar: I think that growing stuff wasn't enough. They had to have meat and you can't grow that.
> Teacher: (Options for responding)
> - Even in an agricultural society, the food from farming wasn't enough. They needed meat as well. (Paraphrases)
> - Why do you suppose they needed meat? (Challenges; asks for hypotheses)
> - I see. Thank you, Tamar. Does anyone else want to comment on what Tamar has told us? (Appreciates Tamar's contribution and shifts gears to ask for other students' contributions to the inquiry)

If the teacher chooses to paraphrase, she will continue the dialogue with Tamar to examine the kinds of food required and how that food was obtained in Zuni society. If she chooses to challenge by asking for hypotheses, she will shift the inquiry to examine what different kinds of foods are needed to subsist. If the teacher terminates her dialogue with Tamar, she continues the examination of what it means to be an agricultural society, but invites contributions from other members of the class.

This kind of discourse requires the teacher's ability to take in observable data from watching and listening, while at the same time choosing an appropriate response from a variety of options. These choices are guided by the teacher's mindful appreciation of the big ideas that drive the inquiry, but also the need to allow children adequate time for reflection of the surface, or observable, data—the gathering of information, before proceeding to the next level of using that information to further understanding. But whichever response the teacher chooses, respect for each student's ideas is clearly manifest, as is time for students to think and to reflect on what they have said. A climate of safety for all students and their statements, without fear of being wrong, are all incorporated in the interactions. These skills combine to form the masterful art of discussion teaching.

Before the discussion begins, teachers may wish to prepare by generating three or four questions that are rooted in the big ideas underlying the discussion, that will focus the discussion on those critical issues to be examined. The "rhythm" of the questions begins with calling for what the students "know"—that is, calling for observations, summaries of events, and the gathering of data. Questions that follow would be more challenging (reaching for deeper meanings), that is, asking for comparisons, interpretations of data, classifying, hypothesizing, and providing examples. Even more challenging questions might follow (knowing how)—for example, asking for the solution of problems, asking about how issues might be decided, asking about potential consequences of proposals, asking for evaluations and judgments to be made. As the discussion evolves, the questions call for deeper, more sophisticated examinations. Making notes of the questions to be used beforehand and keeping them in reach during the discussion is a helpful strategy. Having some questions prepared in advance will help keep the discussion focused and the teacher centered on those big ideas chosen for examination.

Is asking teachers to become masters of the art of discussion teaching unrealistic? Is it beyond teachers' capability to function as artists in this arena of teaching? To believe that is to do teachers a great disservice. There is great artistry in teachers, and there is good reason to believe that, given both information and the means to put that information into practice, teachers will find ways to elevate their interactive dialogue to art.

PART III

Classroom Applications: Thinking Activities in the Curriculum Areas

CHAPTER 5

Guide to the
Thinking Activities

Chapters 6 through 9 present numerous examples of how of teaching for thinking is implemented in the primary, elementary, and middle grades—that is, the *how-to* of teaching curriculum content with an emphasis on thinking in mathematics, science, language arts, and social studies. Teachers can be reassured that these activities and others like them have been tried and used successfully in classrooms across the continent. What's more, the evidence suggests that they do the job of promoting students' understanding of subject matter as well as developing their intelligent habits of mind. It is safe to say that such activities, carried out over time, will enable students to become more thoughtful, more mature, more reflective, and more capable of solving problems and making sound decisions.

Before opening the classroom door to a rigorous program of thinking, teachers need to be aware of certain provisos. The first is that a single activity, used on occasion, whenever there's a spare period with nothing else to do, does not a program make. Second, a thinking skills program must be enduring. One cannot expect results in a week or even a month. Improvement in thinking comes with extended experience, practice, and reflection on practice over time. The data from classroom research studies suggest that 4 to 6 months would be the minimum time to expect to see strong signs of positive results. Being aware of such provisos may be helpful for teachers who are impatient for signs of significant gains.

STARTING POINT: WHAT'S THE BIG IDEA?

Any thinking activity, in fact, any curriculum activity of merit, begins with the question, What's the big idea? Underlying this question is the assumption that the content of each thinking activity—whether it is one of observing and comparing, problem solving, doing a case, carrying out an investigation, examining original documents, or role playing—will lead to deeper understanding of some central, significant issue or issues. For any curriculum activity with an emphasis on thinking, it is essential that the big idea be identified at the outset, so that it serves as a beacon for generating the activity, as well as for guiding and shaping the inquiry. This is light-years away from simply creating an activity in which students fill in blanks, or color pumpkins orange, or add and subtract a page full of numbers—tasks that students can do without having to suffer the pains of deep thought. A curriculum activity that is rooted in the big idea not only identifies the direction of the study, but also illuminates its relevance for serious work. If the big idea is of substance, then the thinking activity will bear fruitful examination. The inquiry will take students' minds somewhere of value. If the idea is not big, but narrow in scope, then there will be limited opportunity to find deeper meanings in the inquiry.

What are big ideas? How would you know one if you met it on a street on a dark night?

Big ideas set the stage for the process of inquiry. They make statements, rather than ask questions. They have relevance. They are ideas that matter. Some contain moral and ethical implications; some deal with current issues; some with historical imperatives, some with major scientific issues, some with inquiry into the fine and performing arts. While they have a clear focus, they also allow for open-ended inquiry. Big ideas may come from curriculum sourcebooks, from the school district curriculum guides, and especially from the standards and benchmarks found in the curriculum frameworks of state departments and ministries of education. They may arise from the concerns of students or teachers or from current events, history, the media, community affairs, textbooks, books taken from the library, or the day-to-day experiences of students. Examples of some big ideas are

- Fabrics are manufactured materials. They may come from natural or synthetic sources.
- Machines make work easier for people.
- Machines need energy to produce movement.
- Various fuel sources produce energy.
- Standard units of measurement are a part of the mathematical language used to make comparisons, design investigations, and interpret results.
- Mammals are one classification of the animal kingdom.
- Understanding nutrition allows people to make better choices about the foods they choose to eat.
- A set is a group or collection of things that are related. A set of things belongs together in some way.
- People work at different kinds of jobs. They work to earn money, which allows them to buy the things they need.
- People write or tell stories to give information, to entertain and amuse, to make us think, and to give us pleasure.

If an idea is too broad in scope, it may be too abstract or cover too much territory to lead to fruitful classroom study. Examples of such "big big ideas" include

- Natural resources are finite.
- Prejudice breeds hatred.
- All sea life is interdependent.
- Culture is learned.
- Animals and plants adapt and change to survive in different environments.

If an idea is too limited, it may focus on bits and pieces of information and not lend itself to substantive inquiry. Examples of such "small" ideas include

- Magnets have two poles, one called north and one called south.
- Unlike poles attract; like poles repel.
- Ice is frozen water.
- Frogs hatch out of eggs.
- 1, 3, 5, 7, and 9 are odd numbers; 2, 4, 6, and 8 are even numbers.
- Blue and yellow when mixed will produce green.

Topics such as apples, bears, health, jobs, magnets, toys, or shells may lead to the development of a big idea, but they are themselves too ambiguous to lead to productive inquiries.

The generation of big ideas requires the teacher's a priori response to the question, "What is it exactly that I want my students to examine in this curriculum area?" When teachers are certain about their answer, this clarity guides the formation of the big idea. Once the big idea is identified and articulated, the thinking activity can begin to be shaped. Teaching to examine the big idea is at the heart of any thinking activity.

As will be noted in the examples presented in Chapters 6–9, each thinking activity begins with the identification of the big idea. It is from this initial point that the activities are fashioned.

PLANNING FOR TEACHING FOR THINKING

As there are many ways to carve a turkey, there are different organizational schemes that teachers may use to include thinking activities in their daily schedules. Some educators advocate a "special time" for thinking (Paul & Elder, 2002; Pogrow, 2005)—a period during the day that is set aside for emphasis on the higher-order skills. The teaching plan I suggest uses an adaptation of the Play-Debrief-Replay curriculum model that has been described in other texts (Wassermann, 2000; Wassermann & Ivany, 1996). Play-Debrief-Replay accommodates the stages of Gathering Knowledge (Play), Promoting Understanding

(Debriefing), and Applying Knowledge (Replay) comfortably within its framework. The model incorporates Raths's higher-order mental operations (Raths et al., 1986), is teacher friendly, does not require any modifications of grade-level curriculum, and is successful in delivering the goals of teaching for thinking (Wassermann & Ivany, 1996). Rather than requiring an addition to the curriculum, *thinking* becomes the vehicle for students to learn the curriculum.

By using this model to teach the grade-level curriculum, teachers can take students through the learning stages of gathering information, making meaning of that information, and using the information in practical ways. The upshot of this structuring is that students increase their knowledge base, deepen their understanding, and learn how to use information in solving problems. Student learning and thinking flourish in this organizational plan.

ABOUT THE ACTIVITIES

Each activity is introduced with a statement of learning goals, which set the road map for what follows. All the parts of the activity are generated from that beginning, so there is a close connection between means (activities) and ends (learning goals). Big ideas are identified next—so that what is to be examined in the activity is clear.

The thinking operations included in the activity are specified, as are the materials required for *Stage 1—Gathering Knowledge*. It will quickly be seen that all Stage 1 activities call for working with a friend or with a small group of students, for as even young children have noted, it's more fun with a buddy. But beyond that, there is greater payoff when students can work together productively, as ideas are spun from one to the other, in a generative, synergistic flow.

Each activity includes examples of debriefing questions that might be used at *Stage 2—Promoting Understanding*. These types of questions call for analyses of what has been observed. Not all these questions need to be used; as in most cases, the teacher is the one who chooses which are appropriate and is certainly encouraged to add others of his or her own choosing. Examples of more challenging debriefing questions are also included—those that work to deepen and broaden students understanding. Again, teachers choose from among these the questions that are more appropriate to the inquiry and to the students' level of understanding.

For *Stage 3—Applying Knowledge*, a list of activities is suggested that require students to apply their knowledge and their understanding to the solving of problems directly related to the inquiry. These activities may be deployed in different ways. Allowing groups of students to make their own choices from the list and then having groups share what they have done with the whole class afterward has proved to be a helpful process for other teachers in the past and provides for freedom of choice, as well as opportunities to share wisdom across the class.

At *Stage 4—Reflecting and Self-Evaluating*, another list of questions and invitations to respond are presented to show how, at this stage, the "what" and the "how" of student learning is evaluated. It will be seen that the reflecting and self-evaluating questions are closely connected with the learning goals and that searching out students' responses will allow for not only student introspection but also tuning into how the work they have done has been productive in achieving the outcomes.

Reflecting and self-evaluating may be done in a whole-class discussion, or as a written exercise, depending on which method, in the teacher's judgment, is likely to produce better results. For each activity, the questions included at the Stage 4 level invite students to reflect on the quality of their work in that particular inquiry. For reflections and self-evaluation on the quality of thinking, teachers may use some or all of the questions below, which apply to all the activities.

- Tell how you see yourself learning to make better observations.
- Tell how you see yourself learning to carry out good investigations.
- Tell how you see yourself learning to suggest good hypotheses.
- Tell how you see yourself learning to come up with good ideas (theories).
- Tell how you see yourself learning to make better decisions.
- Tell about how you see yourself taking more responsibility in your group work.
- Tell about how you see yourself learning to contribute good ideas to the discussions.
- Tell how you see yourself learning to become a better problem solver.
- Tell about where you think you need more help.
- Tell what you think you can do best.
- Tell what you see as your strengths as a learner and as a member of a group.

There is a lot of substance in each of the curriculum activities, and it will be obvious that the whole range of what is to be done would not normally occur in a single day. Once again, the teacher is the best judge of how many days are to be allocated to a given curriculum activity and how long a period of time is to be spent at each stage. It is advised, however, that Stage 2—Promoting Understanding follow Stage 1—Gathering Knowledge without too much delay, so that students can, shortly after gathering information, begin to process the data they have gathered.

Teachers will want to know about the grade levels for which an activity is appropriate, and in response to that anticipated question, I have made suggestions about grade levels for each. These grade-level guidelines are not written in stone but are offered as suggestions. With a tweak here and a nudge there, an activity for a primary grade may be applied at a higher grade and perhaps the reverse is true; a middle school activity may be modified for upper primary use. There is such a range of talents and skills in, for example, the many different Grade 3 classrooms across the country that it is hard to know, with any assurance, what would make a good fit between a particular curriculum activity and a particular class. Here again, it is the teacher's professional judgment that acts as a guide to selecting those activities that are best suited for his or her class.

CHILDREN WORKING IN GROUPS? CAN IT WORK?

I have heard the complaint from teachers that students are not mature enough to work productively in small groups; that they do not know how to behave, let alone conduct inquiries; and that their discussions are "exchanges of ignorance." There is some truth to all of that, because students who lack experience working in self-directed small-group discussions may quickly go off track, may exhibit behaviors that are far from cooperative, and may cause more disruptions than the teacher wants to handle. It is also true that teachers who expect students to work in groups without any advance preparation as "group workers" may find that students working in groups does not work.

Cooperative group work comes with experience that involves orientation, practice, and reflection on practice. Group-work skills do not result, automatically, from a teacher's admonitions to a class to "work cooperatively." After appropriate orientation and practice periods, teachers should expect trial periods of several weeks before the group work takes a more productive turn.

For more effective group work, it is important, initially, that a set of guidelines be developed by the teacher, preferably in concert with the class, and that help be immediately available when groups seem to be faltering. It is also a helpful strategy to call students to examine, after every small-group session, to what extent the group work was successful, and what improvements need to be made for future work.

Expecting that students will work cooperatively without any instruction about guidelines or how to proceed is expecting more than is reasonable. Expecting that students, after orientation, practice, and reflection on action, will succeed is more than reasonable.

ART, MUSIC, AND COMPUTER STUDIES

But what of art? music? computer studies? Are these not important enough to have been included in the applications chapters? Does their absence suggest that they are not worth a teaching-for-thinking approach?

Alas, for the sake of brevity, these areas have not been given their own chapters. It is not because they are unimportant, or because they do not lend themselves to a teaching-for-thinking design. Music, art, and work with computers have, however, found a place in many of the Stage 3 activities in the four content chapters. While this does not give equal time to these important areas, it does not neglect them altogether.

For teachers who wish to use this teaching-for-thinking framework for lessons in art, music, and computer studies beyond what has been included in the curriculum areas, the following suggestions may lead the way to their own curriculum designs:

Art

- Comparing works of art
- Observing masterpieces
- Criticizing works of art
- Observing different art forms (sculpture, collage, mural painting, oil painting, pottery, sketching, junk art, graffiti, watercolor)
- Observing how perspective, line, color, and form are used in art
- Generating works of art in different forms (paintings, sculpture, pottery, masks, collages, murals)
- Creating works of art to represent different historical events
- Observing the use of art in commerce
- Studying cartooning and the appeal of comics
- Studying political cartoons and evaluating their effects
- Studying and creating caricature
- Observing cave art

Music

- Comparing pieces of music
- Noting the different sounds that can be made by a single instrument
- Observing the kinds of sounds produced by several instruments
- Comparing wind, string, and percussion instruments
- Comparing different styles of music
- Studying how music styles have changed over the years
- Studying the relationship between music and dance
- Making musical instruments
- Learning to play music on simple instruments
- Singing
- Making up songs (music and words)
- Studying the great composers
- Studying the role of music in history
- Studying very early instruments and their sounds
- Studying early dances
- Studying musical criticism
- Studying musical idols and their appeal
- Studying traditional music from other countries, ethnic groups

Computer Studies

- Studying the accuracy of information in the blogosphere
- Comparing information on Web sites with library reference tools and newspapers
- Studying writers' biases in Internet postings
- Developing a class Web site
- Generating humanitarian projects to reach out to a wide readership
- Starting up penpal correspondence via e-mail and iChat with children from different geographical areas
- Designing a YouTube presentation
- Using Web-based information to gather and organize data about historical or current events
- Evaluating and judging computer games, computer programs, and computer curriculum resources

BRAIN–MIND RESEARCH AND CURRICULUM ACTIVITIES

The brain is a wondrous thing. A terribly small organ encased safely in the inner recesses of the skull, weighing a mere 2½ pounds in an adult, it is made of cells that process information and retain a treasure chest of memories, dreams, the words of old songs, the names of childhood chums. This organic matter holds the key to human consciousness—to the way the world works. There is little doubt that in the not-too-distant future, the organ's fundamental secret of how matter becomes conscious will be revealed; it will be like unlocking the mysteries of DNA. The work is already being done.

We have come a long way in our knowledge about the relationship between the brain and intelligence from early days when scientists used skull measurements to conclude, authoritatively, whether certain humans were smart or stupid (Gould, 1981). More recent brain-mind research comes from two different, but related, fields:

- *Neuroscience*, which is based in laboratory research and attempts to show how learning changes the physical structure of the brain and with it, its functional organization
- *Cognitive sciences*, which are studies of behavior and learning from a multidisciplinary perspective that includes the fields of anthropology, linguistics, philosophy, computer science, neuroscience, and several branches of psychology

At major research institutions such as the Massachusetts Institute of Technology; the University of Zurich; the University of Cincinnati; the International Brain Research Foundation; and the Princeton Center for the Study of Brain, Mind and Behavior, to name a few, studies of neuron mechanisms underlying higher-order mental functions are being carried out, with special emphasis on brain-related disorders. Thanks to noninvasive imaging technologies, such as PET (positron emission tomology) and MRI (magnetic resonance imaging), neuroscientists are able to observe brain functions in living humans. This field of neuroscience is at the edge of major new discoveries in the elucidation of human brain mechanisms of cognitive and emotional information processing. As for data that would support classroom practices coming from these early studies, caveat emptor should apply with respect to claims that may be premature, at best, and far beyond what the data allow, at worst.

In spite of the tenuousness of the relationship between these research fields and classroom activities, there has been a renaissance of interest in brain-mind research among educators who seek support for constructivist classroom practices that are supposedly rooted in the neurosciences. However, to call these studies brain-mind studies may be deceptive, because data from this field come from observations of behavior and not observations of brain functioning. While we are certain that the brain is engaged as students undertake certain activities and perform in certain ways, we have no evidence to support claims about how the brain does this.

The most frequently cited text in the field of brain-mind research, *How People Learn: Brain, Mind, Experience, and School*, was published by the Commission on Behavioral and Social Sciences and Education, National Research Council (Bransford, Brown, & Cocking, 2000). The commission's purpose was to establish better links between the research findings on the science of learning and actual classroom practice; the book is an exhaustive discussion of studies from the cognitive science field that suggest classroom practices related to improvement of student learning. Even the authors are quick to point out, however, that the research in this field is emergent— which sheds doubt on its relationship to the kinds of classroom practices that do, in fact, engage the brain.

What we do now have are the "neuromarketers" who offer us ways to peer into our brains via an MRI machine so that we may determine whether we are "neurologically wired for certain political, cultural, and social predispositions" (Goldberg, 2008). Although it is tempting to extrapolate far beyond what the data actually allow, to assume that certain teaching strategies and curriculum activities actually do, in fact, feed the mind in brain-enhancing ways, the final chapter on such a relationship has yet to be written.

While we are far from the moment in time when each teacher will be given his or her own MRI as a diagnostic tool to evaluate the extent to which certain curriculum tasks are lighting up amygdala activity in students' ventral premotor cortexes, we can and do have ways to evaluate student gains that result from their work on thinking activities. Studies of student behavior allow us to determine the extent to which students use thinking as a means of addressing practical and theoretical problems. And while these behavioral tools are a far cry from the high-tech and sophisticated lab tools used in studying brain activity, the behavioral tools have a solid history of demonstrating the extent to which students have grown in their abilities as thinkers (Raths et al., 1986). These tools are included in Chapter 11 of this text.

In the high-tech world in which we live, it should come as no surprise that research is currently underway which promises technological breakthroughs to augment our mental facilities through "electronic plug-ins" and genetic enhancement (Coghlan, 2009). The implications of this work in brainpower enhancement through genetic engineering and prostheses may, it is predicted, be common practice in 40 years. But in the meanwhile, researchers suggest that the best methods of brain enhancement lie in the ways in which we educate children. "Given the right environment, most humans have an amazing potential to develop exciting mental capacities" (Coghlan, 2009, p. 43).

THE TEACHER CHOOSES

Do all curriculum experiences have to be designed around the framework presented in this text? Should all classroom activities be of the higher-order type? There are times when a teacher will want students to see a film, just for the beauty or the fun in it. There are times when the teacher will want the children to make pizza and enjoy the process of preparing, cooking, and eating, without subjecting the procedures to detailed scrutiny. There are times to compute algorithms and memorize spelling words; there are times to play games and listen and obey, especially with regard to student health and safety. And there are times to work on thinking skills. Not every classroom activity needs to be, or should be, an activity in which rigorous thinking is applied—to subject every activity to such a burden would be exhausting. Too much may be over the top; too little is likely to have zero result. The teacher is the best judge of which, how, and how much. This is not a case of the more, the merrier, but rather the teacher's considered response to the question, Is this a curriculum experience in which students would benefit from thinking more deeply about the big ideas behind these studies? If that is the case, then developing the curriculum experience around the teaching-for-thinking framework is likely to lead to the kinds of results that the teacher seeks: the search for the meaning of the big ideas and the application of knowledge to solve problems.

CHAPTER 6

Building Habits of Thinking in Mathematics

Measuring, Graphing, Estimating, Studying Fractions, Calculating, and Puddle Jumping

The activities in this chapter demonstrate how mathematical concepts and skills are taught using a teaching-for-thinking approach. In each, students are required to think for themselves, gathering information and using that information with the teacher's guidance to understand and apply the mathematical concepts. Although guidelines are offered for the range of grade levels for each activity, these are only suggestions. The final determination of what is going to work for an individual class is the teacher's professional judgment.

ACTIVITY 1:
SEEING GEOMETRY IN BUILDING STRUCTURES (GRADES 3–8)

Learning Goals

- To give students an opportunity to examine how simple structures are built
- To foster awareness of the relationship between certain geometrical forms and the design principles on which structures are stabilized

Big Ideas

- While constructions appear in different forms (for example, single-dwelling homes, tall buildings, bridges), certain design principles contribute to structural soundness and stability.
- These principles include length of building units, materials used, forming of joints, angles, and overall shape of the structure (among others).
- Triangles are the most stable arrangements in constructions and are seen in virtually all stable structures.

Thinking Operations Included in This Activity

- Observing, comparing, problem solving, generating hypotheses, examining assumptions, evaluating and judging, applying principles, designing projects and investigations

Materials Needed

- Drinking straws; pairs of scissors; a variety of "joiners," such as straight pins, masking tape, paper clips, clay, rulers

Stage 1: Gathering Knowledge

Student activity

Work in groups of four. Use the straws and the joiners to make a stable construction. You may want to construct the frame of a small house, a bridge, a box, a tower, a gazebo, or any other structure. Be prepared to share your ideas about construction in the debriefing.

Stage 2: Promoting Understanding

Sample debriefing questions

- What observations did you make about how a structure is built?
- What observations did you make about the relationship between the length of straws used and the stability of the structure?
- What observations did you make about the joiners in relation to the stability of the structure?
- What observations did you make about the angles of construction in relation to the stability of the structure?
- What observations did you make about the shape of the structure in relation to its stability?
- What, in your view, contributes to the stability of your structure? What data do you have that support that idea?

More challenging debriefing questions

- How come triangles give greater strength to your structure than squares? How do you explain it?
- How might you test the strength of your construction?
- What construction features might be added to give your structure greater support? What theories do you have about this?
- What does your work on this structure tell you about how houses are built?
- What structural features seem to you to contribute to greater structural stability? How did you figure that out?

Stage 3: Applying Knowledge

- Use the information you gathered in your initial investigations to design a doghouse made of timber.
- Design and build a geodesic dome.
- Use the information you gathered about building to design and build a bridge made of straws that would span the distance across a divide between two desks.
- Go on a trip to a building site. Generate a list of questions to ask construction workers about how tall buildings are designed and built.
- Examine houses that are built on sides of cliffs. Make some observations about how these houses are made stable. How are these constructions different from or similar to houses built on flat sites? Using whatever materials you choose, design a construction that is built on the side of a cliff.

Stage 4: Reflecting and Self-Evaluating

Questions for open discussion or written responses

- Tell about what kind of information you gathered about structures from your initial investigations.
- Tell about what you began to understand about how structures are made more stable.
- Tell about how you used that information and understanding in your problem solving in Stage 3.

Questions that call for the examination of the quality of students' thinking for each activity are included in Chapter 5.

ACTIVITY 2: MEASURING LIQUIDS (GRADES K–3)

Learning Goals

- To give students an opportunity to investigate standard units of liquid measurement
- To develop understanding of the relationship between quarts, pints, liters, cups, ½ cups, ¼ cups, tablespoons, teaspoons, ½ teaspoons, and ¼ teaspoons

Big Ideas

- Standard units of measurement are an essential part of the mathematical language used to make comparisons, design investigations, and interpret the results.

Thinking Operations Included in This Activity

- Observing, comparing, interpreting data, problem solving, making decisions, generating hypotheses, evaluating and judging, creating and inventing, examining assumptions, designing investigations

Materials Needed

The following measuring implements, one set for each working group:

- One-cup measure; 2-cup measure; 4-cup measure; 1-liter measure; 1-tablespoon measure; 1-teaspoon measure; ½-teaspoon measure; ¼-teaspoon measure; newspapers to cover the desktops; a small basin of water; small amounts of sugar, salt, flour, other dry ingredients

Stage 1: Gathering Knowledge

Student activity

Work in groups of three of four. Use the measures to find out what you can about the following amounts: 1 cup, 2 cups, 3 cups, 4 cups, 1 liter, 1 tablespoon, 1 teaspoon, ½ teaspoon, ¼ teaspoon. Use the measures to find out which are larger and which are smaller. Use the measures to find out about the differences in the sizes of these measuring tools.

Stage 2: Promoting Understanding

Sample debriefing questions

- What observations did you make about these measures?
- What observations did you make about the sizes of the spoons?
- What observations did you make about the sizes of the cups?
- What observations did you make about the differences between a teaspoon, a ½-teaspoon, a ¼-teaspoon, and a tablespoon?
- What observations did you make about the differences between 1 cup, 2 cups, 4 cups and a liter?

More challenging debriefing questions

- What are some reasons you can think of for why we use measures?
- In what ways do you suppose accurate measurements are helpful?
- How many ways can you think of to figure out how many teaspoons are equal to 1 cup?
- How much is a quart? How did you figure that out?
- How could you use one or more of these measures to measure the height of a chair? The weight of a dog?
- What other kinds of measuring tools do you know about? In what kinds of ways are these tools used? How do you know?

Stage 3: Applying Knowledge

- Use the information you gathered in your initial investigations to figure out how many cups of water a liter measure can hold.
- Use the information you gathered in your initial investigations to figure out the difference between a liter and a quart.
- Use the measurement tools to figure out what's more and what's less:
  — 2½ liters compared to 1¼ quarts
  — 15 tablespoons compared to 36 teaspoons
  — 6 cups compared to 1½ liters
  — 5½ teaspoons compared to 5 tablespoons

Stage 4: Reflecting and Self-Evaluating

Questions to reflect on in either whole-group discussion or in written exercises:

- Tell about the kind of information you gathered about measuring tools.
- How does any of this information help you to understand about how measurements are made?
- How does this information help you to understand about different sizes of measuring tools?
- Tell about how you used your information and understanding to solve the problems in Stage 3.
- Tell about the ways in which these measuring tools are useful; not useful.
- What were some problems you had in figuring out the way these measuring tools are used? How did you deal with those challenges?

Questions that call for the examination of the quality of students' thinking for each activity are included in Chapter 5.

ACTIVITY 3: TAKING MEASUREMENTS (GRADES 1–4)

Learning Goals

- To give students an opportunity to examine different types of standard and nonstandard measuring tools and how they are used in taking measurements.

Big Ideas

- Standard units of measurement are an essential part of the mathematical language used to make comparisons, design investigations, and interpret the results.

Thinking Operations Included in This Activity

- Observing, collecting data, comparing and recording data, making decisions, applying principles, designing investigations, examining assumptions, suggesting hypotheses, evaluating and judging, solving problems

Materials Needed

- Rulers of various sizes, both metric and nonmetric; tape measures, both metal and cloth; rubber bands; string; popsicle sticks; strips of paper; blocks, cutout tracings of a human foot; cutout tracings of a human hand; straws; sticks of various sizes; pencils; crayons; spoons; yarn; scale; measuring cup; balls of different sizes

Stage 1: Gathering Knowledge

Student activity

Work in groups of three or four. Use the measuring tools to find out how you can measure the following:

- Length of the classroom
- Height of three of your classmates
- Size of your hand
- Distance from your classroom to the general office
- Size of a ball
- Weight of a giraffe
- Size of a puddle

Stage 2: Promoting Understanding

Sample debriefing questions

- What observations did you make about measuring the length of the classroom? How did you decide which measuring tools to use? Which tools were better? Which were less good? How did you figure that out?
- What observations did you make about measuring the height of your classmates? How did you decide which measuring tools to use? Which tools were better? Which tools were less good? How did you figure that out?
- What observations did you make about measuring the size of your hand? How did you decide which measuring tools to use? Which tools were better? Which were less good? How did you figure that out?
- What observations did you make about measuring the distance from your classroom to the general office? How did you decide which measuring tools to use? Which tools were better? Which were less good? How did you figure that out?

More challenging debriefing questions

- How does it help us to know that the length of a room is a specific number of meters? yards? feet? How does it help us to know that the distance between two places is a specific number of feet? yards? meters? miles? How does it help us to know the exact weight of a giraffe?
- What observations did you make about measuring the size of a ball? How did you decide which measuring tools to use? Which tools were better? How did you figure that out?
- What observations did you make about how you could weigh a giraffe? How did you decide which measuring tools would do the job? How did you figure out what you wanted to do?
- What are some good ways to measure things that are hard to measure, such as balloons, hands, noses, or puddles of water? What are some ideas you have?
- What do you do when four children measure the height of the door and each of them gets a different answer? How do you explain the differences? How do you figure out who has the correct measurement?
- Which measuring tools give more reliable measurements? How did you figure that out?
- Why do you suppose getting a correct measurement is important? What are your ideas about it?

Stage 3: Applying Knowledge

Use the information you gathered in your initial investigations to measure, or to figure out how to measure, the following:

- Balloon
- Amount of water in a fish tank
- Amount of rainfall during a 1-hour period
- Height of a tree
- Weight of ½ teaspoon of sugar
- Size of a toenail

Stage 4: Reflecting and Self-Evaluating

Questions for whole-class discussion or a written exercise.

- Tell about the kind of information you gathered about making measurements.
- Tell about how you began to understand about the accuracy in measurements.
- Tell about how you used the information you gathered about measuring in your problem solving in Stage 3.
- What were some challenges you faced in making your measurements?
- How did you deal with those challenges?

Questions that call for the examination of the quality of students' thinking in each activity are included for Chapter 5.

ACTIVITY 4: MEASURING AND GRAPHING (GRADES 4–8)

Learning Goals

- To promote awareness of the value of communicating in quantifiable terms that others can understand
- To develop increased skill in using standard units of measure

Big Ideas

- Linear dimensions of objects can be measured.
- Standard units of measure are agreed on by common consent. They help us to understand what we mean.
- Data gathered from measurements are more easily understood when they are presented in certain forms, such as graphs.

Thinking Operations Included in This Activity

- Observing, comparing, problem solving, generating hypotheses, making decisions, evaluating and judging, collecting and organizing data, interpreting data, designing investigations

Materials Needed

- Yardsticks, tape measures, pencils, scissors, string or yarn or both, masking tape, large sheets of newsprint paper

Stage 1: Gathering Knowledge

Student activity

Work in teams of two or three. Working together, measure the heights of all the boys and girls in the class. Then decide together about the kind of graph that might be appropriate to present the data you have gathered. Design the graph and record the data you have collected.

Stage 2: Promoting Understanding

Sample debriefing questions

- What observations did you make when you were measuring the heights of your classmates?

- What observations did you make about the kinds of measuring tools that were better for this job? How did you figure that out?
- What observations did you make about the accuracy of your measurements?
- What observations did you make about the differences in heights?
- What observations did you make about the range of differences in heights among the girls? among the boys?
- What observations did you make about the differences in heights between the boys' group and the girls' group?

More challenging debriefing questions

- How did you determine the accuracy of your measurements?
- What are some reasons for trying to get accuracy in measurement? Why is that important?
- How did you figure out which measuring tools were better for this job?
- How do you explain the variation in heights among the students?
- How do you explain the differences in heights between boys and girls?
- How did you decide on the way to graph your information?
- What makes your graph good?
- If you had to do this activity again, how would you change the way to do it? Tell why you believe that to be a better way.

Stage 3: Applying Knowledge

- Compare your team's graph results with that of another team of students. What differences are you finding in the data you gathered? How do you explain those differences? Whose graph is more accurate? How would you figure that out?
- Design another kind of graph to present your information in a way that is more easily read and understood.
- Design a graph that shows, at a glance, the variations in heights of all the students in the class.
- Design a graph that shows, at a glance, the differences in heights between boys and girls.
- Design a system of measuring heights of students that is *very* accurate.
- Using the data in your graph and, working with your team members, write three statements that you can make that you believe to be positively true about the data you have graphed.

Stage 4: Reflecting and Self-Evaluating

Questions for whole-class discussion or a written exercise:

- Tell about what you have begun to understand about making measurements.
- Tell about what you consider to be your best work in this set of activities.

- Tell about how you used the information you gathered to work on the solving of problems in Stage 3.
- Tell about some of the challenges you faced in solving the problems in Stage 3.
- Tell about how you dealt with those challenges.

Questions that call for the examination of the quality of students' thinking for each activity are included in Chapter 5.

ACTIVITY 5:
ESTIMATING, COLLECTING DATA, AND GRAPHING (GRADES 4–8)

Learning Goals

- To provide students with an opportunity to make informed estimates, gather hard data, graph the data, and compare the data with their estimates

Big Ideas

- Estimation allows us to use comparative data in a more informal way to arrive at conclusions and make decisions.
- Good estimations are helpful in allowing us to make judgments that do not involve laborious computation.
- Estimations are approximations and should be treated as informed guesses.
- Estimations that are not rooted in data may be no more helpful than wild guesses.

Thinking Operations Included in This Activity

- Observing, comparing, collecting and organizing data, interpreting data, problem solving, making decisions, evaluating and judging, examining assumptions

Materials Needed

- Graphing paper, notepaper, class lists

Stage 1: Gathering Knowledge

Student activity

Work in teams of three. Use the class list, and make an estimation of how much time each student spends, on average, playing computer or video games. Talk together and see if you can devise a way of making informed estimates of each student's gaming time. Then create a graph indicating your estimates of each student's gaming time.

Finally, make a survey of each student's average gaming time each day. Create a second graph showing the data you have gathered about actual gaming time for each student.

Stage 2: Promoting Understanding

Sample debriefing questions

- What observations did you use to make your estimates about average video and computer gaming time for each student?
- In your view, to what extent were those observations reliable? How did those observations lead you to informed estimates?
- What observations did you make about the differences in your two graphs? How do you explain those differences?
- What's an estimate? How are estimates helpful in gathering data?
- How might estimates mislead you? How do you know the difference between informed estimates and wild guesses? What are your ideas?

More Challenging Debriefing Questions

- What ideas do you have about making better estimates? What observations might help you in making better estimates?
- What assumptions did you make when making your estimates? What led you to make those assumptions?
- What methods did you use in determining what kind of graph to create in graphing the data for your estimates? for your survey?
- How was that graph helpful? What kind of graph might have been more helpful?
- What were the important similarities and differences in your two graphs?

Stage 3: Applying Knowledge

- Work with a partner. Use the information you gathered in Stages 1 and 2 to make some estimates of how long it would take you to
  — Walk a mile
  — Run around the perimeter of the school yard 3 times
  — Earn $25.00
  — Do 20 math problems
  — Teach a 6-year-old how to tell time

After you have made your estimates, identify the assumptions you made about each estimate. What estimates are more likely to be valid? Which are more likely to be wild guesses? Rethink your estimates as you reconsider the assumptions you have made. Then select one of these problems and gather accurate data on how long it actually takes to do that activity.

Stage 4: Reflecting and Self-Evaluating

Questions for whole-class discussion or a written exercise.

- Tell about the assumptions you made in making your estimates. Where did those assumptions come from?
- Tell about what you now understand about making estimates.
- Tell what you understand about how estimates can be misleading.
- Tell what you understand to be the difference between estimates and data.
- What were some of the aspects of this activity that you think you did well?
- What were some of the challenges for you?
- How do you see yourself learning to make better estimates?

Questions that call for the examination of the quality of students' thinking for each activity are included in Chapter 5.

ACTIVITY 6: MEASURING TIME (GRADES K–3)

Learning Goals

- To provide opportunities for experiences with standard units for measuring time
- To increase appreciation for the usefulness of standard units of measure in communicating our thoughts to others
- To promote awareness of what can be done in different time periods

Big Ideas

- The passage of time can be measured. There are standard, agreed-upon units of measure for hours, minutes, days, months, and years. Our standard units of time are measured by the rotation of the earth around the sun.

Thinking Operations Included in This Activity

- Observing, comparing, interpreting data, examining assumptions, suggesting hypotheses, evaluating and judging, problem solving, making decisions, imagining and inventing, designing investigations, applying principles

Materials Needed

- For each group: a variety of instruments that measure hours, minutes, and days, for example, an hourglass, clocks (digital, analog, windup, alarm, sweep second hand, wall), timers, a stopwatch; a cardboard clock with movable minute and second hands; a calendar; a metronome

Stage 1: Gathering Knowledge

Student activity

Work in groups of four. Carry out some investigations with these instruments that measure time, and make some observations about how time is measured. Do some playing around with these materials and talk to each other about what you have observed about these time-measuring instruments.

Stage 2: Promoting Understanding

Sample debriefing questions

- What observations did you make about these time-measuring instruments?
- What observations did you make about how seconds are measured? minutes? hours?
- What observations did you make about the differences between timers and clocks?
- What observations did you make about the differences between analog and digital clocks? Which are easier for you to tell time? How come?
- What observations did you make about the calendar? How are calendars like clocks? How are they different from clocks?

More challenging debriefing questions

- What do you suppose seconds are? How do you suppose seconds are measured?
- What do you suppose minutes are? How do you suppose minutes are measured?
- What do you suppose hours are? How do you suppose hours are measured?
- What do you suppose days are? How do you suppose days are measured?
- Who do you suppose decided that a day had 24 hours? How did this come about? What are your theories?
- Why do you suppose that all the people in the world use the same time measurements? What are your ideas about it?

- How does measuring time help us in our lives? What are your thoughts about it?
- How does time control our activities? What are your thoughts about it?
- How could you tell what time it was if you didn't have a clock? What would help you in estimating the time? What are you thoughts on it?
- What's a good way to learn to tell time? What are your thoughts on it?
- How do you suppose dogs can tell time? How does a dog know when it's time for you to come home from school? What are your thoughts on it?
- What does it mean when someone says, "Time flies"? What are your ideas?
- What does it mean when someone says, "Time is dragging"? What are your ideas?

Stage 3: Applying Knowledge

Use the materials provided to your group to calculate how long it takes to

- Bounce a ball 100 times
- Drink a glass of water
- Fill a bucket with water
- Run around the playground 3 times
- Grow a flower from a seed
- Walk home from school
- Do a dozen addition problems
- Use the materials provided for Stage 1 to calculate how many minutes there are in a school day.
- Use the materials in the center to calculate how many hours there are in a weekend.
- Make a sundial.
- Create a calendar in which you highlight the birthdays of all the important people in your life.
- Work with a partner and choose a piece of music that you like to listen to. Use the metronome to figure how the time of the music is measured.

Stage 4: Reflecting and Self-Evaluating

Questions for whole-class discussion or a written exercise.

- Tell about what observations you have made about how time is measured.
- Tell about what observations you have made about how time is divided.
- Tell about some of the differences you have seen between clocks and calendars.
- Tell about what was hard for you in this activity.
- Tell about what was easy for you in this activity.

Questions that call for the examination of the quality of students' thinking in each activity are included for Chapter 5.

ACTIVITY 7: MEASURING TEMPERATURE (GRADES 3–8)

Learning Goals

- To provide students with an opportunity to observe and understand about temperature, how it is measured, and the inaccuracies in measurement

Big Ideas

- One way to measure the heat of an object is by taking its temperature. Temperature is measured by instruments called thermometers. Temperatures of the same objects vary under different conditions. Measurements of temperature are subject to human error and to inaccuracies in measuring instruments.

Thinking Operations Included in This Activity

- Observing, comparing, classifying, suggesting hypotheses, examining assumptions, problem solving, evaluating and judging, designing investigations, collecting and organizing data, summarizing

Materials Needed

- A variety of thermometers (indoor, outdoor, body temperature thermometers); a variety of warm, cold, and room-temperature objects (for example, a mug of warm or hot water, ice cubes, a package of frozen food, a glass of juice, a stuffed animal, a piece of cheese, a tomato, an apple, a book, a leaf, a flower, a piece of paper, a flowerpot)

Stage 1: Gathering Knowledge

Student activity

Work in groups of four. Use the thermometers to take the temperature of the different objects that have been given to your group. Have different members of the group take the temperatures of the same objects, using different thermometers. Each one of you record his or her observations about the temperature of these objects. Talk together about the observations you made.

Stage 2: Promoting Understanding

Sample debriefing questions

- Tell me about some of the observations you made about the temperatures of these objects.
- What observations did you make about warm temperatures?

- What observations did you make about cool temperatures?
- What observations did you make about the differences in temperatures measured by the different people of the same object? How do these temperatures vary?
- What observations did you make about the differences in temperatures of the same objects measured by different thermometers? How do these temperatures vary?
- What observations did you make about the way we measure temperature?

More challenging debriefing questions

- What does it mean when something is said to be warm? What are your thoughts about that?
- What does it mean when something is said to be cool? What are your thoughts about that?
- How do you explain the differences in temperatures of the same object, measured by different people? What hypotheses can you suggest?
- How do you explain the differences in temperatures of the same object measured by different thermometers? What hypotheses can you suggest?
- How do you suppose you might change the temperature of an object? What are your ideas?
- How do you suppose the temperature of the weather is measured? What are your ideas?
- What assumptions do you make when you hear, on the radio, that the temperature outside today is 85 degrees?
- What kinds of conditions cause temperatures of objects to rise? To fall? What are some theories you have about that?

Stage 3: Applying Knowledge

- Work with a partner and design an investigation that will compare the differences in temperature of any object taken by two different thermometers. See if you can figure out which thermometer is more accurate.
- Work with a partner. Design an investigation that will measure the temperature of the area outside your school for a period of 2 weeks. Design a graph to record your findings. Talk together about how you might have improved on your gathering of the data and your graphing of the results.
- Work with a partner. Measure the temperature of the area outside your school for a period of 1 week. Compare your findings with the recorded temperature of your town or city listed in the newspapers, on the Internet, or on TV. Talk together and suggest some hypotheses for the differences in temperature measurements.
- Work with a partner. Go to an Internet site that forecasts the

temperature in your town for the next 5 days. Take a printout or copy the forecasted temperatures on a sheet of paper. Then, using your own thermometer, compare the differences between the forecast and the temperature you measured. What hypotheses can you suggest to explain the differences?

- Work with a partner. Using any data source you choose (library resources, specialists in the field, Internet, and so on) find out what you can about global warming. What are some differences in points of view about global warming? See if you and your partner can make a determination, based on the information you have obtained, of whether global warming is a serious threat. Write a short summary of your findings.
- Work with a partner. Make a thermometer that shows temperature in Fahrenheit degrees. Make another one that shows temperature in Celsius degrees. Compare the similarities and differences in the two thermometers.

Stage 4: Reflecting and Self-Evaluating

Questions for whole-class discussion or a written exercise.

- Tell about the information you have gathered about temperatures.
- Tell about the information you have gathered about the way temperatures are measured.
- Tell about your understanding of what cold means. Tell about your understanding of what warm means. Tell about your understanding of what hot means.
- Tell how you used the information about temperatures to solve the problems in Stage 3.
- Tell about the challenges you faced in doing some of the problems in Stage 3.
- Tell about what you think you did well in these activities.

Questions that call for the examination of the quality of students' thinking for each activity are included in Chapter 5.

ACTIVITY 8:
GATHERING INFORMATION FROM A GRAPH
(GRADES 3–8)

Learning Goals

- To give students experiences in observing and interpreting data from a graph
- To become familiar with the ways that graphs are used in the recording of information

Big Ideas

- Graphs are used as a means of recording data that allow us to observe and to make interpretations of those data.
- While graphs may accurately record the data, the interpretations made from the data are subject to human error.

Thinking Operations Included in This Activity

- Observing, comparing, evaluating and judging, interpreting data, classifying, examining assumptions, suggesting hypotheses, designing investigations

Materials Needed

- The Activity Card shown in Figure 6.1 should be duplicated and given to each group of students with the introduction below.

Stage 1: Gathering Knowledge

Student activity

Work in groups of four. Examine the information on the Activity Card and talk together about the observations you have made about the best-selling computer and video games of all time. Talk together and make a list of five statements that you believe to be true, based on the information on the graph.

Figure 6.1. Activity Card—Best Selling Computer and Video Games of All Time

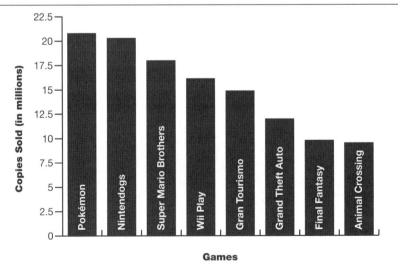

Stage 2: Promoting Understanding

Sample debriefing questions

- What observations did you make about the computer and video games that had the most sales?
- What observations did you make about the kinds of games that sold the most copies?
- What observations did you make about the numbers of millions of copies sold of Super Mario Brothers?
- What observations did you make about the games that sold the fewest copies?
- What observations did you make about the total number of sales of the all time top-selling games?
- What observations can be made about the popularity of video and computer games, based on the numbers of copies sold?

More challenging debriefing questions

- What do the data on the graph tell you about popularity of computer and video games? What assumptions are being made?
- What, in your view, makes a game like Pokémon sell more copies than a game like Animal Crossing? What are some hypotheses you can suggest to explain it?
- Based upon the data on the graph, what kind of computer game would you design that would have a chance of selling a lot of copies? What assumptions have you made?
- What do the data on the graph tell you about the differences between the sales of Pokémon and Nintendogs?
- What do the data on the graph tell you about the differences between the sales of Animal Crossing and Wii Play?
- What information can you not know from this graph about who is buying all these games? What assumptions have you made?

Stage 3: Applying Knowledge

- Work with a partner. Design your own graph showing the kinds of computer games you and two of your friends have purchased in the past year, including the prices of each game.
- Work with a partner. Gather information from the other students in the class to find out which computer games are the most popular among the boys and those most popular among the girls. Make a graph to show the data you have collected.
- Work with a partner. Think about at least five different kinds of data that you could graph that would be helpful to you in your life.
- Work with a partner. Search through newspapers and magazines and cut out different examples of information that is graphed. Talk together and compare the graphs. How are they alike? How are they

different? Which one is more helpful? less helpful? What are some reasons for that?

- Work with a partner and make a survey of the amounts of money spent on computer and video games that students in your class have purchased during the past 6 months. Design a graph showing these expenditures.

Stage 4: Reflecting and Self-Evaluating

Questions for whole-class discussion or a written exercise.

- Tell about the kinds of observations you made about graphs.
- Tell about how you see graphs as useful ways to show information.
- Tell about how the data in graphs are interpreted.
- Tell about your understanding of how you read the data in graphs and what meaning they have for you.
- Tell about how you used the work you did in Stages 1 and 2 to do the problem solving in Stage 3.
- Tell about some of the challenges you faced in this activity.
- Tell about where you think you did your best work.

Questions that call for the examination of the quality of students' thinking for each activity are included in Chapter 5.

ACTIVITY 9: MORE MEASURING AND GRAPHING (GRADES 4–8)

Learning Goals

- To provide students with opportunities to extend their knowledge and understanding of how data are gathered from measurements and how graphs are constructed from those data

Big Ideas

- Standard units of measure enable us to calculate quantities with consistency.
- Measurements are subject to human error and are not infallible.
- One way to record and present data is by graphing.

Thinking Operations Included in This Activity

- Observing, comparing, collecting and organizing data, interpreting data, examining assumptions, evaluating and judging, suggesting hypotheses, summarizing, applying principles to new situations

Materials Needed

- For each group: several balls of different sizes, measuring tools (tape measure, yardstick, ruler), large-size graph paper

Stage 1: Gathering Knowledge

Student activity

Work in a group of three or four. Measure the distance, in feet, yards, and meters, that your group can throw a ball 10 times. Create a graph, and record the data in feet, yards, and meters of each of your throws. Then choose a different-size ball. Repeat the same activity (10 throws) with this different ball and record the data on a different graph, in feet, yards, and meters. Compare the data in both graphs. What are some similarities? What are some differences? How do you explain the differences?

Stage 2: Promoting Understanding

Sample debriefing questions

- What observations did you make about the length of the throws of the first ball?
- What observations did you make about the number of feet that each of you could throw ball number 1? the number of yards? the number of meters?
- What observations did you make about the number of feet that each of you could throw ball number 2? the number of yards? the number of meters?
- What observations did you make about the differences between feet, yards, and meters?
- What observations did you make about the differences in lengths of throw among different members of your group? How did you record those differences on your graph?
- What observations did you make about how graphs are used to present the data you collected?

More challenging debriefing questions

- How did you determine the accuracy of your measurements? How do you know your measurements are accurate? How can you be sure?
- As you look at your graph, how would you summarize the data presented in it?
- In what other ways might you have graphed your data? What other kinds of graphs might have been useful?
- In what other ways, beside graphing, might these data have been illustrated? Why do you suppose that that method is better or less good than putting your data in a graph?
- What other means of measuring the distances might you have used? What can you say about the accuracy of those measures?

Stage 3: Applying Knowledge

- Use the information you gathered in your initial investigations to design a better graph. Give your graph to another team of students

and ask them to interpret the data in the graph according to what you have recorded. What conclusions do they draw from the data?
- Work with the same team of 3–4 students, and using any standard measure and five different-size balls, take turns dropping the balls from the same height. Determine the amount of time it takes for the balls to drop from exactly the same height. Then create a graph and graph the data from your investigations.
- Work with a different team of 3–4 students, and using any standard measure and the same five balls, take turns dropping the balls from a different height and determine the amount of time it takes for the balls to drop. Create a graph and record the data from your investigations.

Stage 4: Reflecting and Self-Evaluating

Questions for whole-group discussion or a written exercise.

- Tell about the information you gathered about standard units of measure.
- Tell about the differences you observed among yards, feet, and meters.
- Tell about what you began to understand about standard units of measurement.
- Tell about what you began to understand about graphing information.
- Tell about what you began to understand about accuracy in measurements.
- Tell how you used the information you gathered in Stages 1 and 2 to do the investigations in Stage 3.
- Tell about some of the challenges you faced with measurements and graphing.

Questions that call for the examination of the quality of students' thinking for each activity are included in Chapter 5.

ACTIVITY 10: MEASURING AREA (GRADES K–4)

Learning Goals

- To promote understanding of the concepts of area and perimeter
- To give students an opportunity to examine the differences between area and perimeter
- To develop skills in calculating area and perimeter

Big Ideas

- The amount needed to cover a surface is its area. The perimeter is the distance around the edge of the surface area. If you want to enclose a region, you calculate its perimeter. If you want to cover the surface, you calculate the area.

Thinking Operations Included in This Activity

- Observing, comparing, problem solving, interpreting data, suggesting hypotheses, examining assumptions, designing projects and investigations, evaluating and judging

Materials Needed

- Large sheets of 1-inch graph paper, cut into different-sized squares and rectangles (for example, 5" x 8", 8" x 14", 6" x 12", 13" x 10"); colored pieces of cardboard or paper, cut into 1" squares and 1" x 2" rectangles; assorted triangle shapes; additional sheets of graph paper; rulers and scissors

Stage 1: Gathering Knowledge

Student activity

Work in groups of three. Use the materials to conduct some investigations about how many cardboard pieces it takes to cover the surface of each of the sheets of paper. What observations can you make about how many colored squares it takes to cover each sheet of graph paper? how many rectangles? how many triangles? Then, use the materials to conduct some investigations to find out how many pieces it takes to go around the edges of these sheets of paper.

Stage 2: Promoting Understanding

Sample debriefing questions

- What observations did you make about the number of colored squares it took to cover the surface of the different sheets of graph paper?
- What observations did you make about the number of colored rectangles it took to cover the surface of the different sheets of graph paper?
- What observations did you make about the number of colored triangles it took to cover the surface of the different sheets of graph paper?
- What observations did you make about the number of colored squares, triangles, and rectangles it took to go around the edges of each sheet of paper?
- What observations did you make about the surfaces that needed more squares? more rectangles? more triangles?
- What observations did you make about the differences among

squares, rectangles, and triangles? What observations did you make about how these different shapes covered the surface of these different sheets of graph paper?

More challenging debriefing questions

- When you look at the surfaces of these sheets of paper, how can you tell which ones have the largest surface areas? What are your ideas about that?
- What might be some other ways to measure the surface area of these large sheets of paper? What are your ideas about that?
- What other ways can you think of to measure the perimeters—the distance around the edge of these sheets?
- What do you see as some differences between the measurements of the area of a sheet of paper and its perimeter? How do you know that is true?

Stage 3: Applying Knowledge

- Use the materials to measure the surface area of the side of a box of cereal. Use the materials to measure the perimeter of the side of the box.
- Use the materials to figure out how much paper you need to cover a library book.
- Use the materials to figure out the surface area of your desk top. Use the materials to figure out the perimeter of your desk top.
- Use the materials to figure out the surface area of a computer screen. Use the materials to figure out the perimeter of the screen.
- Use the materials to figure out the perimeter of the classroom.
- Use the materials to figure out the surface area of the classroom floor.

Stage 4: Reflecting and Self-Evaluating

It is suggested that these reflections be done in a whole-class discussion.

- Tell about what observations you made about measuring surface area.
- Tell about what was difficult about measuring surface area.
- Tell about the observations you made about measuring perimeter.
- Tell what was difficult about measuring perimeter.
- Tell what you understand to be the differences between area and perimeter. Tell what you understand about the differences in measuring each.
- Tell about where you think you need more help.
- Tell about what you think you can do best.

Questions that call for the examination of the quality of students' thinking for each activity are included in Chapter 5.

ACTIVITY 11:
UNDERSTANDING FRACTIONS (GRADES K–3)

Learning Goals

- To give students opportunities to investigate with fractions
- To develop understanding about larger and smaller fractions
- To further understanding that fractions are amounts that represent parts of a whole
- To promote understanding of the notations of fractions and fraction equivalents

Big Ideas

- Fractions are parts of a whole.
- Fractions are used when we want to cut something into pieces or to represent a part of some whole thing.
- Although 24 is larger than 12, the fraction $\frac{1}{24}$ is smaller than the fraction $\frac{1}{12}$.

Thinking Operations Included in This Activity

- Observing, comparing, problem solving, generating hypotheses, examining assumptions, evaluating and judging, interpreting data, designing investigations

Materials Needed

- 12" x 12" sheets of graph paper; rulers; scissors; crayons or felt pens

Stage 1: Gathering Knowledge

Student activity

Work with a partner on this problem.

Problem: Sonja just made this square pizza. She made a square pizza instead of a round one because she thought it would be easier to divide it into 4 equal parts to share with each of her 3 friends. (One piece is for Sonja.) Help Sonja by cutting her square pizza into 4 equal pieces. Use the ruler and the scissors to do this. Make sure that every piece of pizza is the same size! Use the crayons or the felt pen to mark each piece with the fraction ¼—to show that each piece is exactly one fourth of the whole pizza.

Stage 2: Promoting Understanding

Sample debriefing questions

- What observations did you make about the size of each quarter piece of pizza?

- What observations did you make about what you had to do to cut the pizza into four equal parts?
- What observations did you make about how much of the pizza is left when you eat one quarter? when you eat 2 quarters? when you eat 3 quarters?
- What observations did you make about the difference between one quarter and the fraction ¼?

More challenging debriefing questions

- What does ¼ mean to you? What are your ideas?
- What does ½ mean to you? What are your ideas?
- What does ¾ mean to you? How is ¾ different from or similar to ½? How do you know?
- What does ⁴⁄₄ mean to you? How is ⁴⁄₄ different from or similar to one whole? How do you know?
- What would happen if you cut a quarter piece of pizza into two halves? How do you know? What would happen if you cut all the quarter pieces into halves? How do you know? What observations can you make about the number of half-quarter pieces that would fit into the whole pizza?

Stage 3: Applying Knowledge

- Work with a partner. Figure out a way to show in an illustration that ²⁄₈ is equal to ¼.
- Work with a partner. Figure out a way to show in an illustration that ⁴⁄₈ is equal to ½.
- Work with a partner. Figure out a way to show in an illustration that ⅛ is smaller than ¼.
- Work with a partner. Figure out a way to show in an illustration that ³⁄₆ is equal to ½.
- Work with a partner. Draw a large round circle to represent a large pizza. Use your measurement tools to divide this pizza into 6 equal pieces. Tell what you think would be a good label for each of the pieces.

Stage 4: Reflecting and Self-Evaluating

It is suggested that reflecting and self-evaluating for this inquiry be carried out in a whole-class discussion.

- Tell about what you have observed about fractions.
- Tell about what you have observed about how fractions are smaller parts of a whole.
- Tell about what you have observed about how fractions are written.
- Tell about your understanding of what ½ means.
- How come ⅛ is a smaller amount than ¼? How do you explain it?
- Tell about how you used your understanding to work out the problems in Stage 3.
- What was hard for you in this inquiry? What was easy for you?

Questions that call for the examination of the quality of students' thinking for each activity are included in Chapter 5.

ACTIVITY 12:
CONDUCTING INVESTIGATIONS—USING COMPUTERS TO CALCULATE (GRADES 3–8)

Learning Goals

- To give students an opportunity to figure out how to use a computer (or a calculator) to do calculations of addition, subtraction, multiplication, and division

Big Ideas

- Computers and calculators are tools and devices that allow the user to do addition, subtraction, multiplication, and division.

Thinking Operations

- Designing investigations, collecting and organizing data, summarizing, examining assumptions, evaluating and judging, observing, comparing

Materials Needed

- PC or Macintosh computers, or handheld calculators, ideally one for each pair of students

Stage 1: Gathering Knowledge

Student activity

Work in teams of two. Spend some time on the computer locating the tool that allows you to do computations. (A handheld calculator may also be used for this activity.) Then, working together, make up 5 number problems that require you to do addition, subtraction, multiplication, and division (5 problems for each). Use the computer or the calculator to figure out the answers to these number problems.

Stage 2: Promoting Understanding

Sample debriefing questions

- What observations did you make about the calculator in the computer?
- What observations did you make about how a computer or calculator is used to do addition problems? subtraction problems? multiplication problems? division problems?
- What observations did you make about how to locate the calculator in the computer? How would you describe that to a friend?

- What observations did you make about the symbols found on the keypad? What did you find out about those symbols?
- What observations did you make about other calculations that your computer or calculator could do? How did you figure that out?

More challenging debriefing questions

- How can you tell that the answers you got from your calculations were correct? What makes you think that is true?
- Do calculators ever make mistakes? What are your ideas about that?
- How do calculators on a computer compare to pocket calculators? How are they alike? different? Which would serve you better? How come?
- What kinds of errors is a person likely to make when using a calculator to compute answers to number problems? What are your ideas about that?

Stage 3: Applying Knowledge

- Work with a partner. Invent some problems using decimals. Use the computer or the pocket calculator to figure out the answers to those problems. Then try to figure out whether the answers you got were correct.
- Work with a partner. Invent some problems using fractions. Use the computer or pocket calculator to figure out the answers to those problems. Then try to figure out whether the answers you got were correct.
- Work with a partner. Invent a very complicated problem that requires you to add and divide. Use the computer or pocket calculator to figure out the answer to the problem. Then try to figure out whether the answer you got was correct.
- Work with a partner. Write out some clear and simple directions to explain to a much younger student just how to use the computer or pocket calculator. Test out your instructions on a younger student and see if the student can follow them to use either device.

Stage 4: Reflecting and Self-Evaluating

This may be done in whole-class discussion or as a written exercise.

- Tell about what you have observed about using a computer calculator. What were some good things about using this calculator? What gave you some difficulty?
- Tell about what you understand about how these calculators are used.
- Tell how you used that information to do the inquiries in Stage 3.
- Tell about some of the challenges you faced in these inquiries.
- Tell about what you think you can do well.

Questions that call for the examination of the quality of students' thinking for each activity are included in Chapter 5.

CHAPTER 7

Building Habits of Thinking in Science

Investigating Gravity, Weather, Seeds, Machines, and Germs . . . and What About Pluto?

The activities in this chapter provide opportunities for students to examine some big ideas in the science curriculum. Activities are formatted to follow the teaching-for-thinking design: Gathering Knowledge, Promoting Understanding, Applying Knowledge, and Reflecting and Self-evaluating. Grade-level guidelines are suggested for each.

ACTIVITY 1:
STUDYING AIR PRESSURE AND WEIGHT (GRADES 1–4)

Learning Goals

- To promote increased awareness of air pressure and weight
- To promote increased awareness of how air pressure is used as an energy force

Big Ideas

- Air exists even though it cannot be seen.
- Air exerts pressure and occupies space.
- Air has weight.
- Air pressure can be used as an energy force.

Thinking Operations Included in This Activity

- Observing, comparing, collecting and recording data, suggesting hypotheses, examining assumptions, making decisions, designing investigations, applying principles

Materials Needed

- If possible, sets of these materials should be provided for all working groups: balloons of different shapes and sizes; string, straws, balance scale, rubber bands, timer; paper cups, paper clips

Stage 1: Gathering Knowledge

Student activity

- Work in groups of three. Use the balloons and straws to find out what you can about air. Try as many investigations as you can think of to gather your information. Talk with each other about what you have observed.

Stage 2: Promoting Understanding

Sample debriefing questions

- What observations did you make about air?
- What observations did you make about balloons? What observations did you make about straws?
- What observations did you make about how air gets into a balloon? a straw?
- What observations did you make about how air comes out of a balloon? a straw?
- What observations did you make about the weight of air?
- What observations did you make about the force of air when it comes out of the balloon? a straw?
- What observations did you make about how you could use air to move objects?

More challenging debriefing questions

- How did you know that there was air in the balloon? What did you do to find that out?
- How did you know that there was air in the straw? What did you do to find that out?
- How might you be able to weigh air? What investigations did you do to find out that air has weight?
- What investigations did you do to find out that air can be used to move objects? How did you determine that it was the air that did the work?
- In what other ways can air be used as an energy force? What are your ideas about that?

Stage 3: Applying Knowledge

- Design some investigations to show how you could use balloons to lift a paper cup, a piece of paper, a paper clip.

- Design some investigations to show how you might use straws to do the same lifting.
- Design some investigations to show how long air can stay in a balloon. Design some investigations to show how you can increase that amount of time.
- Design some investigations to show some differences between straws and balloons.
- Work with new materials (such as pinwheels, parachutes made with cloth and string, paper cups, and pieces of paper) to find out more about air. Design some investigations to demonstrate what you found.
- Design some investigations to show how we get air to work for us.
- Design some investigations to show how you might weigh air. How might you determine if your measurement was accurate?
- Design some investigations to show how air expands and contracts in relation to temperature.

Stage 4: Reflecting and Self-Evaluating

This inquiry may be done in a whole-group discussion or as a written exercise.

- Tell about the information you gathered about air.
- Tell about how you know that air takes up space.
- Tell about how you know that air exerts pressure.
- Tell about the investigations you conducted to find out more about air.
- Tell about how you saw air used to do work.
- Tell about how you used your information and understanding to design your investigations in Stage 3.
- What did you find difficult in designing your investigations?
- Tell what you think you did best.

Questions that call for the examination of the quality of students' thinking for each activity are included in Chapter 5.

ACTIVITY 2:
STUDYING GRAVITY AS A FORCE (GRADES K–8)

Learning Goals

- To promote awareness of how the force of gravity pulls things down

Big Ideas

- Gravity is a force that you cannot see directly, but you can observe its effects.
- Gravity is a force of nature that explains why objects fall.

- While gravity pulls an object down, the shape of the object will affect the speed of its fall.

Thinking Operations Included in the Activity

- Observing, comparing, interpreting data, suggesting hypotheses, designing investigations, examining assumptions

Materials Needed

- Ideally, sets of these materials should be provided for each working group: many different types of objects that provide an assortment of different weights and shapes, such as blocks, balls, books, papers, pens, pencils, and chalk (anything from around the classroom is useful for these investigations), plus a timer, a scale, a yardstick or meter stick, and paper to record measurements and observations

Stage 1: Gathering Knowledge

Student activity

Work in groups of three or four. Use the materials to design some investigations to observe how things fall. What observations did you make about falling things? What observations did you make about how fast or slowly an object fell? Talk together and try to figure out how and why the objects fall as they do. Use the paper to record your measurements and observations about falling things.

Stage 2: Promoting Understanding

Sample debriefing questions

- Tell about some of the investigations you designed to observe how objects fall.
- What observations did you make about how the objects fell?
- What observations did you make about objects that fell faster? More slowly?
- What other observations did you make about falling objects?

More challenging debriefing questions

- How do you explain why objects fall? How come they just don't lie there in space? What ideas do you have about that?
- What observations did you make about the relationship of the weight of an object to the amount of time it took to fall? How did you figure that out?
- What observations did you make about the relationship of the shape of the object and the amount of time it took to fall? How did you figure that out?

- What do you know about the force of gravity? Where did you get those ideas from?
- What other things are affected by the force of gravity? How do you know that is true?
- How come a heavier object falls at the same speed as a lighter one? How do you explain it?
- What do you suppose keeps a flat sheet of paper afloat longer than a crumpled sheet of paper? How do you explain it? What are your ideas?
- What observations did you make about other forces that influence falling objects besides gravity?

Stage 3: Applying Knowledge

- Design some other investigations using materials of different shapes and weights to study how objects fall.
- Use some cloth and string and make some parachutes. Design some investigations to observe and record how parachutes fall and the effect of the force of gravity on a parachute.
- Make some paper airplanes. Design some investigations to observe and record how paper airplanes are affected by the force of gravity.
- Gather about a dozen balls. Conduct some investigations with the balls to make some observations about how the force of gravity affects the bounce and fall of the balls.
- Using some bubble pipes or straws and a tray of soapy water, make some bubbles. Conduct investigations with the bubbles to make some observations about how the force of gravity affects the bubbles.

Stage 4: Reflecting and Self-Evaluating

This inquiry may be conducted in a whole-class discussion or as a written exercise.

- Tell about the kind of information you gathered about falling objects.
- Tell about what you have observed about the force of gravity on falling objects.
- Tell about what you have understood about how the force of gravity works.
- Tell about what you have observed about how shapes of objects and their weights influence the way they fall.
- Tell what you know about what other objects are affected by the force of gravity.
- Tell how you used the observations you made to help you design your investigations in Stage 3.
- Tell about some of the challenges you faced in carrying out your investigations.

Questions that call for the examination of the quality of students' thinking for each activity are included in Chapter 5.

ACTIVITY 3: GROWING THINGS (GRADES K–4)

Learning Goals

- To promote understanding of how plants are grown from seeds
- To develop appreciation of the role that water, light, and air play in plant growth

Big Ideas

- Many plants grow from seeds formed by the parent plant.
- Many plants are dependent on air, water, light, and warmth to grow.

Thinking Operations Included in This Activity

- Observing, comparing, designing investigations, examining assumptions, suggesting hypotheses, evaluating and judging, making decisions, applying principles, summarizing

Materials Needed

- Several deep saucers, paper towels, water, bean seeds

Stage 1: Gathering Knowledge

Student activity

Work in groups of three. Begin by soaking the seeds in water overnight. The next day, drain and rinse them. Put two or three paper towels into the bottom of each of three saucers. Sprinkle a handful of bean seeds onto the paper in each saucer. Pour only enough water into the first saucer to get the paper towels wet. Pour enough water into the second saucer to fill it up. Leave the third saucer dry. Put the three saucers in a warm place for about 5 days. Keep a close watch every day on what is happening in each saucer. Make some careful notes about your observations for each day. Talk to each other about your observations. At the end of 5 days, observe and compare what has happened to each of the bean seeds in each of the saucers. Be prepared to share your observations in the debriefing.

Stage 2: Promoting Understanding

Sample debriefing questions

- Describe what you did in this activity.
- What observations have you made about the seeds in the first saucer? Describe what you see as clearly as you can.

- What observations have you made about the seeds in the second saucer? Describe what you see as clearly as you can.
- What observations have you made about the seeds in the third saucer? Describe what you see as clearly as you can.
- What differences have you observed in the three saucers? Describe the differences as clearly as you can.

More challenging debriefing questions

- How do you explain what happened in the first saucer? What ideas do you have about it? How do you know that is true?
- How do you explain what happened in the second saucer? What ideas do you have about it? How do you know that is true?
- How do you explain what happened in the third saucer? What ideas do you have about it? How do you know that is true?
- Which of the saucers turned out to be the best place to grow your seeds? What makes you think that is true? What assumptions have you made?
- What do these investigations tell you about what seeds need to grow? What makes you think that is true?
- How important a role does light play in growing seeds? How do you know that it true?
- How important a role does water play in growing seeds? How do you know that is true?
- How important a role does air play in growing seeds? How do you know that is true?

Stage 3: Applying Knowledge

- Work with a partner. Design an investigation in which you try to grow a plant from a potato. Write a plan of what you want to do. Then use what you have written to carry out your plan. Make careful observations about what is happening and make some notes about it.
- Work with a partner. Design an investigation in which you try to grow plants from any of the following: apple seeds, orange seeds, avocado pits, melon seeds, squash seeds, tulip or any other flower bulb, onions, carrots, peanuts (Some children are extremely allergic to peanuts, and if this is the case in your classroom, peanuts should be excluded from this list.)
- Work with one or two partners. Arrange a visit to a nursery, a greenhouse, a farm, or a farmer's market. Prepare a list of questions that you will want to ask the owners or growers about what they do to cultivate and grow their vegetables, plants, and fruits. Make some careful notes or draw some illustrations to show how this is done.
- Work with a partner. Arrange a visit to the fruit and vegetable section of a supermarket. Make a list of what kinds of fruits and vegetables you find there that are grown from seeds and those that are not grown from seeds.

- Work with a friend and use the resources of the Internet to find out what you can about hydroponics—the growing of plants in water. Working together, write a summary about how plants are grown in water and how this is different from growing plants in soil.
- Work with a partner and use the resources of the Internet to find out what you can about how farmers use pesticides to keep pests from destroying their crops. Working together, write a summary about how pesticides are used and their benefits and dangers.

Stage 4: Reflecting and Self-Evaluating

This activity may be done in a whole-class discussion or as a written exercise.

- Tell about your investigations into the growing-plants-from-seeds activity. What are some important things you observed about growing plants from seeds?
- Tell about your understanding of how plants are grown from seeds.
- Tell about how you used that information to solve the problems in Stage 3.
- Tell about the kinds of challenges you faced in designing your investigations. How did you deal with those challenges? Which challenges stumped you? Which were you able to work through?

Questions that call for the examination of the quality of students' thinking for each activity are included in Chapter 5.

ACTIVITY 4: STUDYING SOUNDS (GRADES 3–8)

Learning Goals

- To promote awareness of how sounds are made, how they differ, how they travel, how they are detected, and how they may be varied

Big Ideas

- Whenever sound is produced, something is quivering, trembling, shaking back and forth, and sending vibrations through the air.
- The vibrations caused by sound set sound waves in motion that carry from the sounding object through the air into our ears.
- Three characteristics of sound are pitch, volume, and quality.

Thinking Operations Included in This Activity

- Observing, comparing, suggesting hypotheses, classifying, examining assumptions, making decisions, imagining and creating, designing investigations, collecting and organizing data, evaluating and judging, summarizing

Materials Needed

- A variety of musical and nonmusical instruments, such as flute, recorder, drum set, triangles, whistle, tin can, string, wire, balloons, pots and pans, drumsticks, rattles, shakers, guitar, ukulele, rubber bands, old-fashioned washboards

Stage 1: Gathering Knowledge

Student activity

Work in groups of three or four. Use the materials to produce some sounds. Make careful observations of the kinds of sounds that each object is capable of making. Try some experiments to see how you can vary the kinds of sounds that each makes and record your observations.

Stage 2: Promoting Understanding

Sample debriefing questions

- What observations did you make about the sounds that you could make with each of the objects?
- What observations did you make about how the sound is produced?
- What observations did you make about how you were able to vary the sounds?
- What comparisons did you make about the different sounds produced by the different objects? In what ways were the sounds alike? How were they different?

More challenging debriefing questions

- How are the sounds of triangles different from the sounds of rattles? How are they alike?
- How are the sounds of drums different from the sounds of flutes? How are they alike?
- What do you have to do in order to make sounds from rubber bands? String? Shakers? Flutes? What do you suppose created those sounds? What hypotheses can you suggest?
- What did you do to increase the loudness of the sounds? How do you know that what you did made the sounds louder and softer? How do you know that's true?
- What did you do to vary the pitch of the sounds? How do you know that what you did was responsible for changing the pitch? How do you know that's true?
- Do all of us hear sounds in the same way? What are your ideas about that?

- Which objects make nicer sounds? What do you consider to be a nice sound? How do you explain the difference between nicer and not very nice sounds?

Stage 3: Applying Knowledge

- Work with a partner and listen for all the sounds you can hear in your classroom for a period of 10 minutes. Record your observations about the sounds that you heard. Then, working together, classify the different sounds.
- Work with a partner and make a plastic drum using a piece of plastic and a plastic bowl. Stretch the plastic tightly over the bowl and secure it with a rubber band. Tape the plastic down with some masking tape, to keep it very taut. Place some small beans or paper clips on the top of this drum and beat the drum lightly with a wooden spoon. Observe what happens to the beans or clips when you beat your drum. Make some notes to record your observations. Then suggest some hypotheses to explain why the beans or clips jump when you beat your drum.
- Work with a partner. You will need a comb and a paper napkin or a piece of tissue paper. Wrap the paper around the comb and use it as an instrument to make some sounds. What observations can you make about how the sounds are produced? What observations can you make about what is happening to the paper when you blow on it to make a sound? What hypotheses can you suggest about what is causing the sound to be made?
- Work with a partner. Each of you take turns whistling, while the other observes what happens to the air you are blowing out of your mouth while whistling. How do you vary the pitch, the volume, and the quality of your whistle? Record your observations and suggest some hypotheses to explain how you could vary the sounds of your whistles.
- Work with a partner. Using a large piece of construction paper, design a paper cone that can be used as a loudspeaker. Tape the edges of the paper together to secure it. Take turns while one of you speaks into the cone, and the other makes observations, listening to the differences in the quality, pitch, and volume of the sounds. Write some hypotheses to explain how this works.
- Design an investigation using a small baking pan or sturdy shoe box and about a dozen large rubber bands. Use the materials to make a guitar. Try to make as many different sounds as you can with your guitar. What do you have to do to vary the sounds? How do you explain the difference in the sounds that you produce?
- You will need at least six empty soda or juice bottles for this investigation. Work with a partner and fill the bottles with different amounts of water. Set them in a line and, using a small stick or pencil to tap on the bottles, experiment with the amounts of water

until you can produce a scale of notes. Make up a song that you can play with the sounds from the bottles. Suggest some hypotheses to explain how you can make sounds with water, a stick, and bottles.

- Work with a partner and use the Internet to find out what you can about deafness. What happens when a person loses his or her hearing? Write a summary of your findings.
- Work with a partner and conduct some investigations outside your school to find out about the kinds of noises you hear in the neighborhood. Then, returning to school, classify the sounds you have heard and tell about how each sound affects you.
- Work with a partner and use the Internet to find out what you can about how loud sounds hurt our ears. What did you discover about the importance of noise control?
- Design some investigations to show that some substances carry sound better than others. Make some observations and record your findings.
- Work with a partner and, using any materials you have available, design and construct a model of the human ear.
- Work with a partner and design an investigation to show what determines the pitch, volume, and quality of the sound that a musical instrument can make.

Stage 4: Reflecting and Self-Evaluating

This activity may be done in a whole-class discussion or as a written exercise.

- Tell about some of your observations about how sound is made (about how pitch is varied, and how volume is varied).
- Tell about some of your observations about how sound travels through the air.
- Tell about what you have begun to understand about sound.
- What were some of the challenges you faced while you were designing your investigations? How did you deal with those challenges?

Questions that call for the examination of the quality of students' thinking for each activity are included in Chapter 5.

ACTIVITY 5: STUDYING SIMPLE MACHINES (GRADES K–3)

Learning Goals

- To increase awareness of the variety of simple machines used to make our work easier

Big Ideas

- Simple machines allow us to do work more quickly and easily.
- Simple machines can be used to do all kinds of work, such as lifting, pushing, grinding, chopping, digging, and carrying.

Thinking Operations Included in This Activity

- Observing, comparing, suggesting hypotheses, designing investigations, classifying, collecting and organizing data, looking for assumptions, imagining and creating, making decisions, summarizing

Materials Needed

- A variety of nonfunctioning or discarded simple machines, such as kitchen scales, scissors, staplers, can opener, garlic press, rotary eggbeater, timer, pulley, wheels of all sizes, bicycle, wedges, screws, screwdriver

Stage 1: Gathering Knowledge

Student activity

Work in groups of four. Use the materials to make some observations about these simple machines. Select one or two to take apart. Make some observations of all the parts. Then, working together, make a list of these parts and make some illustrations of them. Then, put the parts together and reassemble the machine.

Team up with another group of four students and compare your lists and illustrations. How are the machines alike? How are they different? How are the working parts alike? How are they different? Talk together about the similarities and differences.

Stage 2: Promoting Understanding

Sample debriefing questions

- What observations did you make about your machines?
- What observations did you make about the parts of the machines?
- How are the parts of the machines different from each other? How are they alike?
- What observations did you make about how the parts help the machine to do its work?
- What observations did you make about how these machines are like some of the playground equipment found in the school yard?
- What observations did you make about how these machines are like some of the machines in your kitchen?

- What observations did you make about how these machines help us to do work?
- What observations did you make about how these machines move or are made to move?

More challenging debriefing questions

- What observations did you make about the machines that use wheels? How do the wheels help to do the work? What makes you think that is true?
- What observations did you make about the machines that use levers? How do the levers help to do the work? What makes you think that is true?
- What observations did you make about machines that use pulleys? How do the pulleys help to do the work? What makes you think that is true?
- What observations did you make about machines with gears? How do the gears help to do the work? What makes you think that is true?
- What observations did you make about machines that use wedges? How do the wedges help to do the work? What makes you think that is true?
- How do you suppose these machines make our work easier? What hypotheses can you suggest to explain it?
- How might our lives be different if we didn't have a wheel to make our work easier? What are your thoughts about that?
- How do you suppose the wheel got invented? What are your thoughts about that?
- How do the different parts of a machine enable it to do its job? What theories can you suggest?
- What do you know about how different people who provide services in your city or town use machines, for example, gardeners, carpenters, firefighters, garbage collectors, recycling collectors, gas station attendants, farmers, bank tellers, supermarket checkout clerks?

Stage 3: Applying Knowledge

- Work with a friend. Find as many pictures of machines as you can (in newspapers and magazines). Cut them out and classify them into groups. Label each group.
- Work with two friends. Do some investigations of different machines found in and around the school. Make some observations to find what makes these different machines move—that is, which machines are moved by electricity? by wind? by water? by springs? by muscles? Make a list of the machines and classify them according to what you think makes them move.
- Get permission to do this from a parent or teacher or both. Work with a friend and visit a building site that is under construction. Observe the different machines that are in use at the building site. Observe the kind of work they do and what kind of force is used to

make that machine operate (for example, electricity, steam, force of muscles). Working together, make some illustrations of these machines, showing the force needed to make the machine operate.

- Work with a friend. Create an illustration that would show how we might build a house without the use of any machines.
- Work with two friends. Design a machine that would do your homework. Make a clear illustration of that machine, showing how it would work.
- Work with a friend to study any computer that you have in your school. Make some illustrations of how you see the computer as a machine that helps you in your work.
- Work with a friend. You will need a knife, a cutting board, a potato (or onion, carrot, or cucumber), and an electric chopping machine. Design an investigation to show the differences in chopping a potato (onion, carrot, cucumber) by hand or by machine.
- Work with a friend. You will need a pulley, some string, and 10 books for this investigation. Design an investigation to show the differences in bringing a load of books up a flight of stairs with a pulley and carrying them up the stairs in your arms. Write or draw about the differences of both methods.
- Work with a friend. Use the Internet to study how automobiles have helped us and also what they do to our environment. Working together, write a summary of your findings.
- Work with a friend. Use the Internet to find out what you can about electric cars and cars that are run on gasoline. Write a short summary that shows the differences in these two different methods of car operation.

Stage 4: Reflecting and Self-Evaluating

This may be done in a whole-class discussion or as a written exercise.

- Tell about what you have begun to understand about machines, about wheels, about levers, about pulleys, about gears, about inclined planes.
- Tell about what you have begun to understand about how machines work.
- Tell about what you have begun to understand about how machines help people to do work.
- Tell what you have begun to understand about the different ways in which machines can be made to work for us.
- Tell what you have begun to understand about the differences to our lives that machines make.
- Tell about some of the challenges you faced in working on these activities. What challenges stumped you? How did you deal with them?

Questions that call for the examination of the quality of students' thinking for each activity are included in Chapter 5.

ACTIVITY 6: STUDYING AIR AND WEATHER (GRADES 3–8)

Learning Goals

- To enable students to gather information about the qualities of air, for example, temperature, humidity, pressure, movements, and other characteristics that combine to make the weather
- To increase awareness of the human impact on air quality

Big Ideas

- The sun, the air, and water play leading roles in weather conditions such as hurricanes, thunderstorms, snowstorms, heat waves, cold spells, humidity, and fog.
- Changes in air conditions determine the weather.
- While some atmospheric conditions are beyond human control, some conditions are directly affected by what we do on the earth's surface to alter the atmospheric conditions.

Thinking Operations Included in This Activity

- Observing, evaluating and judging, classifying, comparing, collecting and organizing data, examining assumptions, suggesting hypotheses, designing investigations, summarizing, making decisions, interpreting data

Materials Needed

- Access to Internet.

Stage 1: Gathering Knowledge

Student activity

Work with a partner. Use the classroom computer to find the following link: www.weathermap.us/

Make some observations about what you see in the weather map. What observations can you make about the different weather conditions that are shown? What observations can you make about how a forecast can be made about the weather from the data in the map? What observations can you make about how the conditions in the map have changed since the previous day? What do the data in the map tell you about the movement of the air? The temperatures in various locations? The changes in weather that are expected?

Then look out the window and compare what you see outside to the information in the map that shows the weather in your town or city.

Stage 2: Promoting Understanding

Sample debriefing questions

- What observations did you make about the weather in various locations in the United States and Canada?
- What observations did you make about the locations where it was raining? snowing? foggy? windy? where there were thunderstorms? the direction of the wind?
- What observations did you make about the temperature in various locations of the United States and Canada?
- What did you observe about the high and low pressure systems marked with *H* and *L*?
- How did your observations of the weather on the map for your town or city compare with what you saw outside the classroom window?
- What observations can you make in the weather map that would tell you about tomorrow's weather?

More challenging debriefing questions

- What's air? How do you know it's up there? What are your ideas about it? What evidence do you have to support your ideas?
- What do you suppose makes the weather humid? How do you explain it? What theories do you have?
- What makes the weather hot? How do you explain it? What theories do you have?
- What role does the wind play in changing weather conditions? What theories do you have?
- Where do you suppose snow comes from? How do you explain it? What theories do you have?
- Where do you suppose rain comes from? How do you explain it? What theories do you have?
- Where do you suppose fog comes from? How do you explain it? What theories do you have?
- What have you heard about global warming? What does that mean to you?
- In what ways do we, as humans, affect changes in the weather? What are your ideas about that? How do you know that is true?

Stage 3: Applying Knowledge

- Work with a partner. Observe cloud formations over a period of 1 week to discover changes in cloud formation from time to time. Record your findings. Suggest some hypotheses to explain why the clouds change.
- Work with a partner. Using an outdoor thermometer, observe the outside temperature for a period of 1 week. Record your findings.

Then suggest some hypotheses to explain the reasons for these temperature changes. Compare your findings with the recording of the temperature in the daily newspaper or weather channel. How do you explain the differences in temperature readings?

- Work with a partner. Use the Internet to find out what you can about Hurricane Katrina. Make some observations about how the hurricane was formed and what kinds of force it exerted on the land and on the people. Observe some of the photographs of the area after the hurricane hit. Write a summary statement about what you have learned about hurricanes.
- Work with a partner. Use the Internet to find out what you can about cyclones. How are cyclones different from hurricanes? How are they formed? What weather conditions lead to the formation of cyclones? What kinds of damage do cyclones do? Write a summary statement explaining what you have learned about cyclones.
- Work with a partner. Use the Internet to find out what you can about tornadoes. How are tornadoes different from hurricanes and cyclones? How are they formed? What weather conditions lead to the formation of tornadoes? What kinds of damage do tornadoes do? Write a summary statement explaining what you have learned about tornadoes.
- Work with a small group and divide the work to investigate how snow, rain, and fog are formed. Write a summary of the similarities and differences in these weather conditions.
- Work with a partner and use the Internet to gather data about global warming. What is global warming? What do the data tell you about whether this is a serious threat to our planet Earth? What conclusions can you draw from the data you have gathered?
- Work with a small group of classmates and generate a list of weather sayings that you have heard or have used yourselves (such as "It's raining cats and dogs"). Then write a summary statement to explain how these descriptions of the weather got started and why we keep using them.
- Work with four friends to write a small skit to dramatize how weather affects how we feel.

Stage 4: Reflecting and Self-Evaluating

This may be done in a whole-class discussion or as a written exercise.

- Tell about what you have begun to understand about the relationship between air and weather.
- Tell what you have begun to understand about temperature, humidity, air pressure, wind—the various conditions that make up the weather.
- Tell what you have begun to understand about the role of the sun in contributing to the weather.

- Tell what you have begun to understand about the earth's atmosphere.
- Tell what you have begun to understand about the various weather conditions, for example, snow, rain, humidity, heat waves, fog, cold spells.
- Tell what you have begun to understand about extreme weather conditions, such as hurricanes, tornadoes, cyclones.
- Tell what you have begun to understand about global warming.
- What were some important things you learned about the weather in these activities?
- Tell what you think you did best.
- Tell where you see yourself needing more help.

Questions that call for the examination of the quality of students' thinking for each activity are included in Chapter 5.

ACTIVITY 7: STUDYING ROCKS (GRADES 1–8)

Learning Goals

- To promote awareness of the various kinds of rocks that are found on the earth's surface
- To elevate awareness of where rocks come from, their many different forms, and how they are formed

Big Ideas

- We study rocks to learn about the history of the earth.
- Rocks are formed in several ways: by the cooling of extremely hot materials, by the cementing together of small fragments of soil, or by the changing of rocks into new forms.
- Rocks, while appearing to be very hard, can actually be worn down by forces such as running water and wind.
- The earth's soil is made up of the wearing down of rock.

Thinking Operations Included in This Activity

- Observing, comparing, classifying, suggesting hypotheses, collecting and organizing data, examining assumptions, designing investigations, interpreting data, imagining and creating, summarizing

Materials Needed

- A large collection of stones and rocks (these can be gathered by students from vacant lots, the countryside, or backyards in preparation for this inquiry), photographs of mountains, a bag of soil, photographs of volcanoes

Stage 1: Gathering Knowledge

Student activity

Work in groups of four. Make some observations of the rocks and the soil. Working together, examine the ways in which they are alike and how they are different. Make some notes to describe the similarities and differences. Then decide together how to classify them into groups. Label the groups. When you have finished classifying the rocks and the soil, study the groups and make some further observations of how the rocks are alike and how they are different.

Then observe the photos of the mountains and volcanoes. How do the mountains and the volcanoes fit into any of your categories? How do they compare with the rocks and the soil? Suggest some hypotheses to explain the relationship between rocks and mountains.

Stage 2: Promoting Understanding

Sample debriefing questions

- What observations did you make about the rocks you studied? How would you describe them?
- How are your rocks alike? How are they different? What theories do you have to explain the differences you observed?
- What observations did you make about the soil? How is the soil different from the rocks you observed? How is it similar?
- What observations did you make about the photos of the mountains and volcanoes? How are mountains and volcanoes related to rocks? What theories do you have about that?

More challenging debriefing questions

- Tell about some of the categories you created with your rocks. How are the rocks in each category alike? What kinds of labels did you make for each category?
- Where do you suppose rocks come from? What hypotheses can you suggest that would explain how they are formed?
- Where do you suppose soil comes from? What hypotheses can you suggest that would explain how soil is formed?
- How do you suppose mountains are formed? What hypotheses can you suggest that would explain how mountains are formed? What assumptions have you made?
- How do you suppose the sizes and shapes of rocks can be changed? What hypotheses can you suggest that would explain how the sizes and shapes of rocks can be changed? What assumptions have you made?
- Why do you suppose we study rocks? What do you suppose we can learn from the study of rocks? What hypotheses do you have about that?

Stage 3: Applying Knowledge

- Work with a partner. Gather some soil samples and add some water to it to make a little mud. Form the mud into little balls. Allow the mud balls to harden and observe the results. Compare your "rocks" with the ones you observed in the first stage of this inquiry.
- Work with a partner. Gather some samples of sand. Make some observations about the sand. How is sand different from soil? How is it similar? Suggest some hypotheses to explain how sand is formed and where it comes from.
- Study some photos of deserts. (You can find photos of deserts in library books or on the Internet.) Where do you suppose all that sand came from? How come it formed in these places? Suggest some hypotheses to explain it.
- Work with a partner. Take a walk around your town or city. Observe the different uses of rock in the building of homes, apartments, offices, streets, sidewalks, shops, and steps. Make some notes about the kinds of rock you have observed in the building of your town, city, or school.
- Work with a partner. Use the library or the Internet to locate some photos of mountain ranges, such as the Rockies, the Alps, the Himalayas. Make some observations of how the mountains are shaped, the peaks, the valleys, the slopes. Use the information you gathered in your observations to draw some illustrations of mountains.
- Work with a partner. Use the library or the Internet to locate some photos of the Grand Canyon, with the Colorado River down in the valley between the sides of the canyon walls. What observations can you make about the walls of the canyon? What observations can you make about the river below? How do you suppose the walls of the canyon were formed by that river? What hypotheses can you suggest? What assumptions have you made?
- Work with a partner. Design an investigation to show how water acts on rocks to wear them down. Make some observations of what happens and how.
- Work with a partner. Design an investigation to show how erosion affects certain areas in your town or city.
- Work with a partner and design an investigation to demonstrate how the study of rocks can teach us about the history of the earth.
- Work with a partner and use the library or the Internet to investigate how the eruption of volcanoes creates rocks. Write a summary of what you have discovered.

Stage 4: Reflecting and Self-Evaluating

This may be done in a whole-class discussion or, for intermediate grades, as a written exercise.

- Tell about what you have grown to understand about where rocks come from.
- Tell about your understanding of how rocks are formed.
- Tell about what you have observed about the differences in different kinds of rocks.
- Tell about your understanding of how rocks are worn down.
- Tell about your understanding of how soil is formed from rock.
- Tell about how you used the information you gathered in your investigations to work on the inquiries in Stage 3.
- What were some challenges you faced in designing your investigations?
- How did you deal with those challenges?
- Tell where you think you need more help.

Questions that call for the examination of the quality of students' thinking for each activity are included in Chapter 5.

ACTIVITY 8: STUDYING HOW FOODS SPOIL (GRADES K–8)

Learning Goals

- To promote understanding of the conditions under which food spoils and how the changes occur

Big Ideas

- Certain foods undergo change when they are allowed to decay.
- Preservatives are used to delay the spoiling of foods.
- Organic foods do not make use of preservatives or pesticides.

Thinking Operations Included in This Activity

- Observing, comparing, classifying, collecting and organizing data, examining assumptions, suggesting hypotheses, evaluating and judging, designing investigations, making decisions, imagining and creating, summarizing, applying principles to new situations

Materials Needed

- Small quantities of a variety of foods, for example, flour, sugar, salt, apple, milk, bread, fruits (apple, orange, peach, cherries, grapes, banana), vegetables (potato, carrot, onion, lettuce, tomato, cucumber), potato chips, cheese, dry beans, rice, crackers, butter, soda pop, egg—enough samples so that each pair of students can have at least five different samples of food to study; paper towels; newspapers; plastic knives; magnifying lenses; scales

Stage 1: Gathering Knowledge

Student activity

Work with a partner and make some observations of the foods. Place each sample of food on a paper towel and label it. Write your observations on a sheet of paper, recording the date on which you made your first observation. Observe your food samples over a period of 2 weeks, recording each day the changes you have found in each of the food samples. When you have completed your 2-week study of the samples, talk together about the changes you found in the foods and make a summary of your findings.

Stage 2: Promoting Understanding

Sample debriefing questions

- What observations did you make about the foods you investigated?
- What happened to the samples over the 2-week period?
- What observations did you make about the foods that spoiled more quickly? More slowly? How do you explain that?
- What observations did you make about the foods that didn't spoil?
- Why do you suppose these foods spoiled? How do you explain it?
- Why do you suppose those foods did not spoil? How do you explain it?

More challenging debriefing questions

- What might be done to keep food from spoiling? What hypotheses do you have about that?
- What are some differences between food that has some preservatives and food that is organic? What are your ideas?
- Why do you suppose preservatives are good? What's not so good about using preservatives to keep food fresh? What are your ideas? What data support them?
- Why do you suppose people should pay more money to buy organic food? What are your thoughts about that?
- How can you tell if pesticides have been used to preserve your food? Where can you get that information? What are your ideas about it?
- When foods decay, some of them give off a bad smell. Where do you suppose that smell comes from? What's your theory about that?
- How can you be sure the food you are eating is safe to eat? What's your theory about that?

Stage 3: Applying Knowledge

- Work with a partner and design an investigation to study where the food we eat comes from.

- Work with a partner and use the Internet to make some studies of what pesticides are used for certain foods and what the data say about those pesticides.
- Work with a partner and design an investigation to study the kinds of preservatives that are used in all the foods that each of you eats in a single day.
- Work with a partner and visit a grocery store or supermarket. Talk to some of the workers at the store to find out what they do to keep their fresh foods from spoiling. Write a summary of what they do. Find out what they do with foods that spoil. Write a summary of that as well.
- Work with a partner. Design an investigation to find out what you can about how foods are preserved in canning, boxing, and other packaging methods.
- Work with a partner. Design an investigation to find out what you can about the various ways we have to prevent foods from spoiling. Write a summary of what you have discovered.

Stage 4: Reflecting and Self-Evaluating

This may be done as a whole-class discussion or as a written exercise.

- Tell about your understanding of the ways in which food spoils, about the conditions under which food spoils more quickly, about the conditions under which foods spoil more slowly.
- Tell about your growing understanding of what happens to food when it spoils. What were you able to see happen? What did you smell?
- Tell about your understanding of what is used to keep food from spoiling.
- Tell about your understanding of the difference between food that contains preservatives and food that is organic.
- Tell about the challenges you faced in these inquiries.
- Tell where you think you need more help.

Questions that call for the examination of the quality of students' thinking for each activity are included in Chapter 5.

ACTIVITY 9:
STUDYING BLOOD CIRCULATION (GRADES 4–8)

Learning Goals

- To promote understanding of how the blood circulates in the human body

- To further understanding of the role of the heart in the circulation of the blood
- To promote understanding of the blood as a system that distributes food and oxygen to all the cells in the body

Big Ideas

- Blood moves around the body in a continuous closed circuit of arteries, veins, and capillaries.
- The heart serves as a pump to move the blood through this circulation system.
- Food and oxygen are moved by the blood to all the cells of the body, thus providing nourishment that enables us to grow and be healthy.

Thinking Operations Included in This Activity

- Observing, comparing, summarizing, collecting and organizing data, examining assumptions, suggesting hypotheses, designing investigations, interpreting data, making decisions, applying principles to new situations

Materials Needed:

- A large-scale illustration of the human circulatory system. See, for example,
  http://www.ama-assn.org/ama/pub/category/7152.html
  http://catalog.nucleusinc.com/enlargeexhibit.php?ID=4528
  http://uimc.discoveryhospital.com/main.php?t=symptom&p=anatomy_explorer

Stage 1: Gathering Knowledge

Student activity

Work in a small group of about three or four students. Study the illustration of the circulation system and make some observations of what you can see. Talk together about how you see the system of veins, arteries, and capillaries carrying the blood throughout the body. Talk about your observations of what the heart is doing in relation to the veins and arteries. Be prepared to share your ideas in the debriefing.

Stage 2: Promoting Understanding

Sample debriefing questions

- What observations have you made about the circulatory system?

- What observations did you make about what the heart does in the circulatory system?
- What observations did you make about where the blood travels in the body?
- What observations did you make about how the blood travels from place to place?

More challenging debriefing questions

- Where do you suppose the blood comes from? What are your theories about it?
- What do you suppose are the reasons that blood circulates in this way? What assumptions are being made?
- What do you suppose "circulation" means? What are your ideas about that?
- What are some differences between veins, arteries, and capillaries? What do you make of the functions of each of these vessels?
- How do you suppose the heart does the pumping of blood? How does this work? What ideas do you have about that?
- Why is blood important? What theories do you have about that?

Stage 3: Applying Knowledge

- Work with a small group and make your own illustration of the circulatory system. Be sure to include all the important parts of this system.
- Work with a small group. Use whatever materials you can find to make a working model of the circulatory system. Be prepared to demonstrate to the rest of the class just how this works in the human body.
- Work with a partner and do some investigations on the Internet of the role of the heart in the circulatory system. Write a summary or draw an illustration of your findings.
- Work with a partner and do some investigations on the Internet or in the library of how the blood carries food and oxygen to the cells of the body. Write a summary of your findings.
- Work with a partner and do some investigations on the Internet or in the library of how the blood in the body regulates the body's temperature. Write a summary of your findings.
- Work with a partner and do some investigations on the Internet or in the library of how the white corpuscles in the blood fight disease. Write a summary or draw some illustrations of your findings.
- Take a trip to the Red Cross blood bank in your town or city and find out how volunteers give blood, how it is stored in the bank, and what it means to have a blood transfusion. Write a summary or draw some illustrations of your findings.
- Work with a small group of classmates to do some investigations of

what to do if a classmate is injured and bleeding. Write a summary of your findings.

- If you can obtain some slides of blood cells, look through a microscope and make some observations of what you can see in these cells. Make some diagrams of your observations that show the structure of these cells.
- Work with a partner and take each other's pulse, by placing the two fingers of your hand (forefinger and middle finger) on the blue vein in your wrist that you can see through your skin. Use a second hand on a watch or clock and record each other's pulse rate. Then change partners and do these investigations again. Experiment with doing some exercises and observing how, when your heart is beating more rapidly, your pulse readings change.
- Work with a partner and do some investigations, listening to each other's heartbeat, using a stethoscope. Record your findings. Do some exercises to increase your heart rate and observe the changes.

Stage 4: Reflecting and Self-Evaluating

This inquiry may be done in a whole-class discussion or as a written exercise.

- What understanding do you now have of the circulatory system?
- What understanding do you now have of how the circulatory system carries blood throughout the body?
- What understanding do you now have of the job of the heart in the circulatory system?
- Tell about what you understand about veins, arteries, and capillaries.
- Tell what you understand about how oxygen and food is carried by the blood to all the cells in the body.
- What were some challenges you faced in your investigations? How did you deal with them?
- Tell what you think you can do best.
- Tell where you think you need more help.

Questions that call for the examination of the quality of students' thinking for each activity are included in Chapter 5.

ACTIVITY 10:
STUDYING THE PRESERVATION OF WILDLIFE (GRADES 4–8)

Learning Goals

- To promote understanding of the differences in values between commercial ventures leading to profit and money making, and the preservation of wildlife

Big Ideas

- There is a growing tension between societal forces that wish to preserve wildlife and those who seek to use wildlife for profit and commercial gain.
- The poaching of wildlife results in the diminishing and eventual extinction of numbers of animal and bird species.
- Commercial opportunists believe they have right to trade in wildlife for profit and commercial gain.

Thinking Operations Included in This Activity

- Observing, interpreting data, comparing, suggesting hypotheses, examining assumptions, designing investigations, summarizing, evaluating and judging, creating and imagining, making decisions, applying principles to new situations, collecting and organizing data

Materials Needed

- The mini-case, below, with sufficient copies for all group members.

  "Two dollars a paw! That's what I get for killing a black bear! I know that it's illegal to do this, but what can I do? Why shouldn't I make a profit from this business? I need the extra money to buy what my family and I need to live. So who cares if there's one black bear less in this world? The forests are full of them. Sure, it's against the law. But they have to catch me first, don't they?"

  The illegal trade in wildlife is very profitable—more than $10 billion dollars a year! No wonder poachers are pouring into some countries from all over the world to capture, kill, and sell wildlife.

  The price for one serving of bear paw soup in a restaurant is $1,000. And if you wanted to buy a smuggled orangutan, you could have one for $10,000.

  What is this illegal trading in wildlife doing to the ecology of the areas in which it is going on? Steve Jones, a naturalist, says, "This is big business, but it is destroying the wildlife of many areas and some species are in danger of being completely wiped out. But who is going to speak for the animals when such huge profits are at stake?"

Study Questions

- What do you know about poaching?
- What do you suppose are some reasons that explain the illegal trade in animals, both living and dead?
- What do you see as some consequences of the illegal trade in wildlife?
- What, do you suppose, is so exciting about eating bear paw soup? Why do you suppose anyone would pay $1,000 for a bowl of this soup?

- What is your view about protecting wildlife from illegal poaching? Why, in your view, should wildlife be protected?
- What should governments do to protect the wildlife in their countries? What ideas do you have about this?

Stage 1: Gathering Knowledge

Work in groups of six. Read the case and talk together about your observations of what is happening in the story. Then, working together, develop some responses to the study questions.

Stage 2: Promoting Understanding

Sample debriefing questions

- What observations did you make about illegal poaching of wildlife from reading and discussing this case?
- What observations have you made about the reasons for poaching?
- What observations did you make about the potential profits from poaching?
- What observations have you made about the consequences of poaching for wildlife?
- What observations have you made about the kinds of animals that are prey for poachers?
- What observations have you made about the reasons that people wish to own or eat illegally obtained animals?

More challenging debriefing questions

- Who is right? The poachers who want to make a profit? or those who want to protect and preserve wildlife from being wiped out? What are your thoughts on this?
- Why do you suppose people get a kick out of eating bear paw soup? What's the big deal about that? What are your ideas on it?
- Why do you suppose someone who lives in the city would want to buy and keep an orangutan for a pet? What's so hot about that? What are your ideas about it?
- What do you think kids can do to protect wildlife in their country? Is there a role for children to play in this matter? What are your ideas?
- What do you think governments should do to protect wildlife? What are your ideas?
- What might we do to try to persuade people not to buy illegally obtained wildlife for their own purposes? What are your ideas about that?

Stage 3: Applying Knowledge

- Work with two partners. Use the information you obtained in Stages 1 and 2 to design a survey to find out what the students in your school think about the illegal buying and selling of endangered animals. Design a chart to show the results of your survey and summarize your findings in a brief paragraph.

- Work with a partner and together write a letter to your representative in the national legislature to protest against illegal poaching in your country. Be sure your letter contains good information and presents your ideas in a thoughtful and logical way.
- Work with a partner and use your favorite Internet search engine to find out what you can about animal species that are diminishing in numbers and those who are nearly extinct. Write a summary of your findings.
- Do some investigations and find out what you can about how illegal trade in endangered animals occurs. How do the animals get into your country? How are they sold? What prices are charged for what animals? What are the profits? Draw some illustrations that present the information you have gathered.
- Work with a few partners and create some posters to raise awareness in your school of illegal poaching and what students in the school might do about it.

Stage 4: Reflecting and Self-Evaluating

This may be done in a whole-class discussion or as a written exercise.

- Tell about the information you have gathered about illegal poaching.
- Tell about your understanding of animals that are endangered species.
- Tell about your position about this kind of trade in animals. Where do you stand on these issues?
- Tell about your understanding of both points of view in this animal trade.
- Tell about why you think we should care about this.
- What were some challenges you faced in doing this case study inquiry?
- How did you deal with those challenges?
- Tell about how you are learning to use the Internet to search for information.

Questions that call for the examination of the quality of students' thinking for each activity are included in Chapter 5.

ACTIVITY 11: WHAT IS SCIENCE? (GRADES 4–8)

Learning Goals

- To promote understanding that there is disagreement among scientists about what is true, that science is dependent on intelligent interpretation of data, that there is room for error in science

Big Ideas

- Science is not a bunch of facts to be memorized but a process for producing knowledge.
- Scientists produce knowledge through intelligent examination of evidence and intelligent interpretations of the findings of that evidence.
- Change in scientific knowledge is inevitable because new observations may challenge long-held theories.
- Even leading scientists may disagree about the way evidence is interpreted and, consequently, their findings may differ about what is true.

Thinking Operations Included in This Activity

- Observing, comparing, collecting and organizing data, examining assumptions, suggesting hypotheses, evaluating and judging, designing investigations, summarizing, imagining and creating

Materials Needed

The mini-case below with sufficient copies for all group members.

For more than 75 years, scientists who study the planets and stars agreed that our solar system had 9 planets. As we all know, these planets are Mercury, Venus, Earth, Mars, Jupiter, Saturn, Uranus, Neptune, and Pluto. Scientists came to these conclusions from their studies of the universe using high-powered telescopes, which allowed them to make careful observations of what was out there in the universe.

But in science, new information, based on new observations, may change what we have always believed to be true. In August 2006, there was a meeting of the International Astronomical Union where scientists had a very long and heated argument about the planet Pluto. Finally, the scientists at the meeting decided that Pluto should no longer be included in the list of planets. They claimed that Pluto did not meet their standards of what a planet is. They said it was too small and it behaves in too odd a way to be called a planet. According to their new definition, a "planet is round; it orbits the Sun and has cleared its orbit of competing bodies." Pluto, the scientists said, "just did not meet those standards." Consequently, they invented a new description for Pluto. They called it a "dwarf planet." As a result of their discussions at this meeting, Pluto was kicked off the list of planets in our solar system.

This caused great furor around the world, as many other scientists did not agree with this decision. They responded by saying, "If it's a dwarf planet, it's still a planet! So never mind them! We will still list Pluto on *our* charts as a planet."

Study Questions

- How, according to your knowledge, are scientific discoveries made?
- What kinds of data do scientists have to show in order for us to be sure that a new discovery is really true?
- What happens when scientists disagree?
- How are we to know what to believe?

Stage 1: Gathering Knowledge

Student activity

Work in groups of four, and read, together, the news story. Then talk together about what this story means to you. After you have discussed the events in the story, discuss your responses to the Study Questions that follow the story.

Stage 2: Promoting Understanding

Sample debriefing questions

- What observations did you make about how the scientists at the meeting decided to kick Pluto off the list of planets in our solar system?
- What observations did you make about why the other scientists wanted to keep Pluto in the solar system?
- What observations did you make about the differences in positions between the two groups of scientists?
- What observations did you make about how each group came to their conclusions?
- What observations did you make about how scientists gather information and draw conclusions?

More challenging debriefing questions

- How would you compare the different positions of the two groups of scientists? How are the positions similar? How are they different?
- Where, in your view, does scientific information come from? How do scientists gather information? How do you know that is true?
- What happens when scientists disagree? What are your views on that?
- How come scientists disagree? What hypotheses can you suggest to explain that? What assumptions have you made?
- How come scientific information can change? How do you explain that? What assumptions are you making?
- If scientists disagree, how can we know what is true?

Stage 3: Applying Knowledge

- Work with a partner and use an Internet search engine to find out about one or two scientific discoveries in the past that have been found to be inaccurate or just plain wrong. Write a summary of those discoveries that have now been shown to be wrong.

- Work with a partner and conduct an interview with a scientist or with someone who is working in a science laboratory. Prepare a list of questions for that person to learn how scientific information is gathered and interpreted. Then, after your interview, write a summary of your findings.
- Work with a partner and use the library or an Internet search engine to find out what you can about Dr. Ludwig Semmelweiss, the doctor and scientist who made an important discovery about the relationship between germs and disease. How do you explain the resistance of his fellow doctors and scientists to Semmelweiss's discoveries? Write a summary statement that describes what Semmelweiss found and how the scientific establishment responded to his discoveries.
- In 1910, Halley's comet appeared in the sky. It was regarded by thousands of people as an omen of disaster. These people were terrified that the end of the world was near and they were in a terrible panic! They thought that the comet's tail would sweep over the earth and cover it with poisonous gases, which would kill everyone on planet Earth. No scientist could convince them that their fears were unjustified. Work with two partners and talk together about some of the naive beliefs that some people hold about scientific truths and how they came to those beliefs. Talk also about why scientific evidence does not help to change people's naive beliefs about what they think is true. Write a summary statement of your understandings or draw some cartoons to demonstrate them.

Stage 4: Reflecting and Self-Evaluating

This may be done in a whole-class discussion or as a written exercise.

- Tell about your growing understanding of how scientific data are gathered.
- Tell about your growing understanding of how scientists can disagree about what is true.
- Tell about your growing understanding of what science is.
- Tell about your understanding of how new data are introduced in science and how theories can change.
- Tell about some challenges you faced in any parts of these activities.
- How did you deal with those challenges?

Questions that call for the examination of the quality of students' thinking for each activity are included in Chapter 5.

ACTIVITY 12: GERMS MAKE YOU SICK! (GRADES 4–8)

Learning Goals

- To promote understanding of the role of germs in disease and other illnesses
- To further understanding that germs are living microorganisms that invade the body

Big Ideas

- Most diseases are caused by microbes that invade the body. A more familiar term for these microbes is "germs."
- Germs can enter the body through the air we breathe; through eating food or drinking water; through breaks in the skin, or through the bite of a carrier.
- When we understand more about how germs are spread, it helps us to prevent disease.

Thinking Operations Included in This Activity

- Observing, suggesting hypotheses, examining assumptions, classifying, collecting and organizing data, interpreting data, summarizing, creating and inventing

Stage 1: Gathering Knowledge

Student activity

Work with two partners and make a survey of everyone in the class who has had one or more of the following symptoms of illness in the last month: fever, sore throat, cough, sneezing, cold, rash, vomiting, bellyache, or another illness that has caused absence from school.

Create a graph to show which classmates have had one or more of these symptoms of illness.

Find out what these students did for their illnesses and write a summary of the different remedies they used to help them get well.

Stage 2: Promoting Understanding

Sample debriefing questions

- What observations did you make about the different kinds of illnesses that have been going around your classroom in the last month?

- What observations did you make about the illnesses that occurred more frequently?
- What observations did you make about the numbers of students in your class affected by illnesses?
- What observations did you make about what the students did to help themselves get well again?

More challenging debriefing questions

- How do you suppose people get colds? What are some explanations for it?
- Where do you suppose germs come from? What are your theories? What assumptions are you making?
- What do you know about different kinds of germs? Where do these ideas come from? What assumptions are you making?
- What do you know about how germs come into our bodies? What are your theories about it? What assumptions are being made?
- How do people try to prevent catching a sickness caused by germs? What ideas do you have about that? What assumptions are being made?
- What do you know about the kinds of illnesses that are caused by germs? How do you know that is true? What assumptions are being made?
- How does washing hands help in the prevention of germs being passed from one to another? What are your theories about it? What assumptions are being made?

Stage 3: Applying Knowledge

- Work with a partner. Use the library or the Internet to gather the information you need for this activity. Create a poster of your own design that describes four different kinds of germs: virus, bacterium, fungus, protozoa
- Work with a partner. Create a poster of your own design that describes how your classmates can take precautions against spreading germs. Give your poster a catchy title.
- Work with two partners and use the Internet to find out what you can about diseases that are caused by germs. Write a summary of your findings.
- Work with a partner and use the library or the Internet to find out what you can about two scientists who played major roles in identifying germs as the cause of disease: Semmelweis and Lister. Working together, write a summary that describes the contributions of each of these scientists.
- Work with two partners and use the library or the Internet to find out what you can about the Black Plague. Working together, write

a summary about the causes of the disease, how it spread, what happened to the people who caught it, and what was done to prevent it from spreading.

Stage 4: Reflecting and Self-Evaluating

This may be done in a whole-class discussion or as a written exercise.

- Tell about your growing understanding of the role of germs in disease.
- Tell about your growing understanding of what germs are and what they do to make you sick.
- Tell about your growing understanding of how germs are spread and what we can do to prevent the spread of disease.
- Tell about how you used your growing understanding to carry out the activities in Stage 3.
- Tell about some of the challenges you faced in any of these activities.
- Tell about how you dealt with those challenges.

Questions that call for the examination of the quality of students' thinking for each activity are included in Chapter 5.

Building Habits of Thinking in Language Arts

Reading, Writing Down, Listening, Talking

The activities in Chapter 8 are examples of how curriculum content in the language arts is taught with an emphasis on higher-order thinking. The activities encompass a variety of language arts experiences and are appropriate for elementary- through middle-grade levels.

ACTIVITY 1: STUDYING PUNCTUATION (GRADES 2–4)

Learning Goals

- To promote understanding of the role of punctuation marks and capitalization (commas, capital letters at the beginning of sentences, question marks, exclamation points, colons, and periods) in providing signals to a speaker in translating text to speech
- To promote understanding of how punctuation serves as an aid in reading for meaning

Big Ideas

- Good punctuation is a set of signals that shows the reader how to read the flow of words as a speaker would say them.
- Punctuation signals enable a reader to make clear the meaning of the text.

Thinking Operations Included in This Activity

- Observing, comparing, classifying, evaluating and judging, making decisions, imagining and creating, suggesting hypotheses, applying principles to new situations

Materials Needed

The two pizza stories, with sufficient copies for all students.

Pizza Story 1

do you know how to make pizza you have to make some dough then you have to roll out the dough into a big big circle and put the circle of dough onto a pizza pan next you get some sauce and put sauce all over the top of the dough when you have put the sauce on the dough you have to put some cheese on top of it but first you have to grate the cheese so that you can spread it evenly over the pizza and so that it is easy to melt if you want you can put mushrooms or sausage too some kids even like pineapple on their pizza when you have put all the toppings on you put the pizza into a very hot oven a hot hot oven it takes about 30 minutes to finish baking when it is done you can share it with your friends because you should have about eight big pieces

Pizza Story 2

Do you know how to make pizza? You have to make some dough. Then you have to roll out the dough into a big, big circle and put the circle of dough onto a pizza pan. Next, you get some sauce and put sauce all over the top of the dough. When you have put the sauce on the dough, you have to put some cheese on top of it. But first you have to grate the cheese so that you can spread it evenly over the pizza and so that it is easy to melt. If you want, you can put mushrooms or sausage too. Some kids even like pineapple on their pizza! When you have put all the toppings on, you put the pizza into a very hot oven—a hot, hot oven. It takes about 30 minutes to finish baking. When it is done, you can share it with your friends because you should have about eight big pieces.

Stage 1: Gathering Knowledge

Student activity

Work in groups of four. Silently read the first story about making pizza. Then have one student read it out loud. Make some observations of what you have heard. Ask the person who read the story to make his or her observations of the story. When you have finished making your observations, have another person read the second pizza story. Then compare the first pizza story with the second pizza story. How are the stories alike? How are they different? Make some notes to record the differences.

Stage 2: Promoting Understanding

Sample debriefing questions

- What observations did you make about Pizza Story 1 story when you read it silently?
- What observations did you make about Pizza Story 1 story when it was read aloud?
- What observations did you make about Pizza Story 2?
- What differences did you observe between the Pizza Story 1 and Pizza Story 2?

More challenging debriefing questions

- What were some problems you had when you listened to Pizza Story 1? What do you suppose explains those problems?
- How does a period help you to understand the meaning of the text? What are your ideas?
- How does a comma help you to understand the meaning of the text? What are your ideas?
- How does a capital letter help? What are your ideas?
- What do you see as some reasons for using a comma? period? a capital letter?
- How does punctuation help a reader when he or she is reading a story? What are your ideas?

Stage 3: Applying Knowledge

- Work with a partner and, together, read the little story below. Decide how it should sound, and then use periods, question marks, commas, and exclamation points so that the story makes more sense when it is read aloud.

    last night i watched a movie on tv it was very good because it was so exciting i love movies that tell stories about adventures

- Work with a partner and, together, write a little story about a TV program that you hated. Make sure you use commas, periods, question marks, exclamation points, and capital letters so that when the story is read out loud, the reader knows how to read it correctly.
- Work with a partner. Read the following pairs of sentences and make some observations about the differences in the meanings of each that are the result of different punctuation. Write a summary of your observations.

    He likes pizza.   He likes pizza?
    Put on your sweater.   Put on your sweater!
    You ate the pie.   You ate the pie?

That's finished!	That's finished?
She ate the whole thing!	She ate the whole thing?
Call the cat, June.	Call the cat June.

- Work with a partner. Choose a library book that you both enjoy. Take turns reading several pages of the story aloud to each other. Make some observations of the kinds of punctuation that the author has used in the pages you read. How does the punctuation help you to understand the meaning of the story? Try to pretend that the punctuation has been erased and read two different pages without them. What do you see as some differences? Write a short summary of your observations.
- Work with a friend and make a list of all the different kinds of punctuations you can find in two or three pages of your favorite story. Make a record of these and see if you can describe what they are and how they are used.
- Work with a partner and write some sentences that can be punctuated in different ways to indicate different meanings.

Stage 4: Reflecting and Self-Evaluating

This may be done in a whole class discussion or as a written exercise.

- Tell about your growing understanding of the use of punctuation marks in written work.
- Tell about your understanding of how using different punctuation marks leads to different meanings in a sentence with the same words.
- Tell about what you have understood about the use of commas, question marks, periods, exclamation points, and capital letters.
- What were some challenges you faced in doing these activities?
- How did you deal with those challenges?

Questions that call for the examination of the quality of students' thinking for each activity are included in Chapter 5.

ACTIVITY 2:
STUDYING WORLD ANALYSIS SKILLS—SHORT VOWEL SOUNDS
(GRADES 1–3)

Learning Goals

- To promote understanding of the use of phonic clues in decoding words
- To provide practice with short vowel sounds

Big Ideas

- Phonic clues help us to decode unfamiliar words.
- Short vowel sounds are often heard between two consonants in single syllable words.
- There is no perfect correlation in English words between the sounds of letters and how they are spelled and read in words.

Thinking Operations Included in This Activity

- Observing, comparing, interpreting data, collecting and organizing data, looking for assumptions, applying principles, suggesting hypotheses, judging and evaluating

Materials Needed

- Five individual strips of paper, with the following words in vertical columns:
  a: fat, mat, sat; fan, man, ran; had, bad, sad; rag, tag, bag
  e: set, bet, let; beg, leg, peg; hen, men, then; bed, led, fed
  i: sit, bit, lit; big, pig, jig; pin, fin, tin; lid, bid, rid
  o: box, fox, sox; hot, dot, got; log, fog, jog; job, rob, mob; cod, nod, pod;
  u: but, cut, rut; rug, lug, mug; bun, fun, run

Stage 1: Gathering Knowledge

Student activity

Work in groups of four and observe the lists of words on each of the five sheets of paper. What observations can you make about the words that have an *a* sandwiched between the first and last letters? What observations can you make about the words that have an *e* sandwiched between the first and last letters? What observations can you make about the words that have an *i* sandwiched between the first and last letters? What observations can you make about the words that have a *u* sandwiched between the first and last letters? Make some notes to record your observations.

How do the words on each sheet compare with each other? How are they alike? How are they different? Make some notes to record your comparisons.

Stage 2: Promoting Understanding

Sample debriefing questions

- What observations did you make about the words with the short vowel sound *a*?

- What observations did you make about the words with the short vowel sound *e*?
- What observations did you make about the words with the short vowel sound *i*?
- What observations did you make about the words with the short vowel sound *o*?
- What observations did you make about the words with the short vowel sound *u*?

More challenging debriefing questions

- What similarities did you observe in the words on each sheet?
- What differences did you observe in the words on each sheet?
- What observations can you make about the kinds of words in which short vowel sounds are heard?
- What other words can you think of that would fit onto any of these word ladders? What makes you think that's a good fit?
- Based on these word ladders, what rule can you make about which words take a short vowel sound?

Stage 3: Applying Knowledge

- Work with a partner and create a word ladder using the ending *all*. Try to think of as many words as you can for this ladder and make sure that you can pronounce each of the words.
- Work with a partner and find a library book you enjoy. Read together through a page of the story and identify all the words you can find that use the short vowel sound *a*. Make a list of those words.
- Work with a partner and create a word ladder using the ending *ell*. Try to think of as many words as you can for this ladder and make sure that you can pronounce each of the words.
- Work with a partner and find a library book you enjoy. Read together through page of the book and identify all the words you can find that use the short vowel sound *e*. Make a list of those words.
- Work with a partner and create a word ladder using the ending *ill*. Try to think of as many words as you can for this ladder and make sure that you can pronounce each of the words.
- Work with a partner and find a library book that you enjoy. Read together through a page of the story and identify all the words you can find that use the short vowel sound *i*. Make a list of those words.
- Work with a partner and create a word ladder using the ending *ull*. Try to think of as many words as you can for this ladder and make sure that you can pronounce each of the words.
- Work with a partner and find a library book that you enjoy. Read together through a page of the story and identify all the words you can find that use the short vowel sound *u*. Make a list of those words.

Stage 4: Reflecting and Self-Evaluating

It is suggested that this activity be done in a whole-class discussion.

- Tell what you have observed about the short vowel sounds of *a, e, i, o,* and *u.*
- Tell what you have observed about the words in which a vowel takes a short sound.
- Tell about the words that you have observed that do not take the short vowel sound, that surprised you.
- Tell about how your understanding of the short vowel sounds helped you in decoding new words.
- Tell about how you used your understanding of short vowel sounds in your problem solving in Stage 3.

Questions that call for the examination of the quality of students' thinking for each activity are included in Chapter 5.

ACTIVITY 3:
STUDYING WORD ANALYSIS SKILLS—LONG VOWEL SOUNDS
(GRADES 1–3)

Learning Goals

- To promote understanding of the use of phonic clues in decoding words
- To provide practice with long vowel sounds in single syllable words that end with a silent *e*

Big Ideas

- Phonic clues help us to decode unfamiliar words.
- When an *e* appears at the end of a single-syllable word, with a short vowel sandwiched between two consonants (for example, p-a-n) the *e* is silent but has the affect of changing the vowel from short to long (p-a-n-e).
- While the rule of the silent *e* helps to decode many single-syllable words, it does not apply to all single-syllable words that end in *e.*

Thinking Operations Included in This Activity

- Observing, comparing, suggesting hypotheses, applying principles, summarizing, classifying, examining assumptions, collecting and organizing data, interpreting data, creating and imagining

Materials Needed

Five individual strips of paper with the following words side by side, in vertical columns:

Short a to long a

fat	fate
mat	mate
hat	hate
rat	rate
pan	pane

Short e to long e

Pet	Pete

Short i to long i

rid	ride
hid	hide
dim	dime
din	dine
fin	fine
pin	pine

Short o to long o

cod	code
nod	node
rod	rode
not	note
rot	rote
tot	tote
ton	tone

Short u to long u

tub	tube
cub	cube
dud	dude
cut	cute

Stage 1: Gathering Knowledge

Student activity

Work with a buddy and make some observations of the words in each column. What observations can you make about those words? Compare the words in Column 1 to the words in Column 2. What observations can you make about their similarities and differences?

Stage 2: Promoting Understanding

Sample debriefing questions

- What observations did you make about the words containing the vowel *a* in Column 1?
- What observations did you make about the words containing the vowel *a* in Column 2?
- What observations did you make about the words containing the vowel *e* in Column 1?
- What observations did you make about the words containing the vowel *e* in Column 2?
- What observations did you make about the words containing the vowel *i* in Column 1?
- What observations did you make about the words containing the vowel *i* in Column 2?
- What observations did you make about the words containing the vowel *o* in Column 1?
- What observations did you make about the words containing the vowel *o* in Column 2?
- What observations did you make about the words containing the vowel *u* in Column 1?
- What observations did you make about the words containing the vowel *u* in Column 2?

More challenging debriefing questions

- How are the words containing the vowel *a* in Columns 1 and 2 similar? How are they different?
- How is the word containing the vowel *e* in Columns 1 and 2 similar? How is it different?
- How are the words containing the vowel *i* in Columns 1 and 2 similar? How are they different?
- How are the words containing the vowel *o* in Columns 1 and 2 similar? How are they different?
- How are the words containing the vowel *u* in Columns 1 and 2 similar? How are they different?
- What observations did you make about what happens to the sound of the vowel in each of the columns when the *e* is added at the end of the word? How do you explain it?

Stage 3: Applying Knowledge

- Work with two partners. Write some other columns of words where you can see the short vowel sound changing to a long vowel sound when you add the silent *e*.

- Work with two partners. Write some other columns of single syllable words with a short vowel sound that begin with consonant blends, such as *bl* and *cr* and *fl*. Show how some or all of the short vowel sounds in these words change to a long vowel sound when you add the silent *e*.
- Work with a partner. Invent a game in which you can practice the rule of the silent *e*.
- Work with a partner. Select two pages from your favorite story and pick out all the single-syllable, short vowel sound words. Make a list of them. Then pick out all the single-syllable words that end with a silent *e*. Make a list of them.

Stage 4: Reflecting and Self-Evaluating

This may be done in a whole-class or small-group discussion.

- Tell about the observations you made about how short vowel sounds become long vowel sounds when there is a silent *e* at the end of a word. Tell about your understanding of how this works.
- Tell about how you used that information and understanding in your work in Stage 3.
- What were some challenges you faced in your work in Stage 3?
- Where do you think you need more help?

Questions that call for the examination of the quality of students' thinking for each activity are included in Chapter 5.

ACTIVITY 4:
WRITING OUT—LEARNING TO WRITE CAPTIONS (GRADES K–8)

Learning Goals

- To promote understanding of how the big ideas in images are translated into a few selected words
- To provide practice in encapsulating the important content of images

Big Ideas

- Captions identify and reveal the key aspects of an image.
- Captions are summaries of the content of an image.

Thinking Operations Included in This Activity

- Observing, comparing, summarizing, suggesting hypotheses, examining assumptions, evaluating and judging, interpreting data, making decisions, creating and imagining, applying principles to new situations

Materials Needed

- A collection of photographs that children bring from home; images cut from newspapers and magazines. Each group should have about six photographs to examine.

Stage 1: Gathering Knowledge

Student activity

Work in groups of four. Look at the photographs or illustrations and talk together about the observations you've made in each. Then, working together, decide on what you think would be a good caption (title) for each photograph or illustration. Make sure your caption tells what you think is most important about the photograph. Then paste the photograph or illustration on a sheet of paper and write the caption underneath.

Stage 2: Promoting Understanding

Sample debriefing questions

Have the groups of children show their captioned photographs, one at a time, and ask that the captions be read aloud.

- What are you observing about this photograph?
- What seems to you to be most important in this photograph?
- How do you see the caption of this photograph telling you what is important?
- What other ideas do you have for captioning this photograph? What makes you think that is a good idea?

More challenging questions

- How can you tell if a caption is good? How can you tell if it tells what is important in the photograph?
- What do you look at when you decide about a good caption for your photograph?
- How do you figure out, from your observations, what's important to include in your caption and what to leave out?
- What kinds of photographs or other pictures make for good captions? What kinds of photographs are not easily captioned? What are some differences between these two types of images?

Stage 3: Applying Knowledge

- Work with a partner and collect some other photographs or pictures. Write more captions for these.
- Work with a partner and compare your captions with those of

another pair of students. Give feedback to each other about how your captions can be improved.

- Work in a group of three or four. Make some observations about the captions used for photos and illustrations in a newspaper or magazine. Which captions do you believe tell the best story about the image? Tell why you think those are good captions.
- Work with a partner. Choose at least five books that you have read and decide together how the title of the book is a good caption for the story. Working together, think up another title (caption) for the story that would work as well in giving students a good idea of what that story is about.
- Work in a group of four. Draw some cartoons and write captions for each. Then, exchange your cartoons with those of another group. Give each other feedback about how the captions of the cartoons might be improved.
- Work with a partner and draw some pictures of people who seem to be talking to each other. Draw balloons over their heads and write some captions to indicate what they are saying to each other. Then, exchange your pictures and captions with another pair, and give each other feedback about how the captions might be improved.

Stage 4: Reflecting and Self-Evaluating

This may be done in a whole-class or small-group discussion or as a written exercise.

- Tell about your understanding of how captions work to tell small stories of images.
- Tell about how you go about choosing good words to create captions.
- Tell about how you know your caption is a good one.
- Tell about how you identify what's important in a photograph or an image.
- Tell what you find difficult about writing good captions.
- Tell about where you thought you did your best work in writing captions.
- Tell where you think you need more help.

Questions that call for the examination of the quality of students' thinking for each activity are included in Chapter 5.

ACTIVITY 5: STUDYING WORDS THAT HAVE POWER (GRADES 1–8)

Learning Goals

- To develop appreciation for the power of words to help and to hurt
- To promote understanding of how some words are used in interpersonal communication to build positive feelings about self and how others are used to diminish feelings about self

Big Ideas

- Words have power. They have the power to make you feel good, and they have the power to hurt.
- Words have the power to make you feel liked and accepted and understood. They also have the power to make you feel that nobody cares about you.
- It's important for friends to talk to each other with kindness. It's important for friends to talk to each other without being hurtful.
- Being a good friend means being sensitive to each other's feelings.

Thinking Operations Included in This Activity

- Observing, comparing, collecting and organizing data, examining assumptions, suggesting hypotheses, evaluating and judging, interpreting data, making decisions, applying principles to new situations, creating and inventing, designing investigations

Materials Needed

One or more of the following statements printed on individual sheets of paper or index cards.

- You're stupid.
- Get out of here.
- Nobody likes you.
- You look nice today.
- You can't come to my party.
- I'm so happy to see you.
- You can't play on our team.
- You can't run fast enough.
- You're the best player on the team.
- I will miss you when you go.
- You forgot your lunch? Don't worry. I'll share mine with you.

Stage 1: Gathering Knowledge

Student activity

Work with a group of three or four. Read the student statements on the cards and talk about each of them. Tell about the kinds of words that you consider to be kind. Tell about the kinds of words you consider to be hurtful. What observations can you make about the kinds of words that have power to be kind and those that have power to be hurtful? Working together, make a list of those words (helpful; hurtful). Add any other words to the list that you believe can be used to be kind and those that are used to be hurtful.

Stage 2: Promoting Understanding

Sample debriefing questions

- What observations have you made about words that have power to be kind to others? What words did you include in your "helpful" list?
- What observations have you made about words that have power to be hurtful to others? What words did you include in your "hurtful" list?
- What words did you add to your helpful list? What makes you think that those words are helpful?
- What words did you add to your hurtful list? What makes you think that those words are hurtful?

More challenging questions

- Why do you suppose people use words to hurt each other? What's behind it? What ideas do you have?
- How should you respond when someone says something hurtful to you? What ideas do you have about that? What do you see as some consequences of that response?
- How should you respond when someone says something kind to you? What ideas to do you have about that? What do you see as some consequences of that response?
- How do you see hurtful words as the start of something even more hurtful—such as fights? How does that happen? What ideas do you have?

Stage 3: Applying Knowledge

- Work with a partner and try to remember some times when classmates or other kids were being hurtful to you on the playground or in class. What did they say? Make a list of the words they used that were very hurtful.
- Work with a partner and try to remember some times when classmates or other kids were being very kind to you on the playground or in class. What did they say? Make a list of the words that they used that were most kind and made you feel really good.
- Work with three or four friends and try to create a plan to eliminate cruel and hurtful comments in the classroom and on the playground. Be prepared to tell why you think your plan will work. Get some feedback from other groups about how you might improve your plan.
- Work with a partner and write a list of a dozen sentences that you believe to be most hurtful to others. Write another list of a dozen sentences that you believe to be most kind to others.

Stage 4: Reflecting and Self-Evaluating

This may be done in whole-class discussion or as a written exercise.

- Tell about your growing understanding of how words are used to be hurtful to others.
- Tell about your growing understanding of how words are used to be kind to others.
- Tell about your growing understanding of what's behind the use of words that are hurtful to others.
- Tell about some consequences you see of using words that are hurtful to others.
- What do you see as some of your best work in these activities?
- Where do you see yourself needing more help?

Questions that call for the examination of the quality of students' thinking for each activity are included in Chapter 5.

ACTIVITY 6:
COMMUNICATING CLEARLY (GRADES 3–8)

Learning Goals

- To promote the use of clarity in learning to say what you mean
- To further understanding of the need for clarity in expressing ideas

Big Ideas

- Expressing your ideas clearly makes what you say and what you mean more easily understood.
- Clear, intelligent, and responsible talking is a very important part of interpersonal communication.

Thinking Operations Included in This Activity

- Observing, comparing, classifying, summarizing, examining assumptions, suggesting hypotheses, evaluating and judging, making decisions, designing investigations, applying principles to new situations

Materials Needed

A collection of cards for each group with examples of less-than-clear communications between students, for example:

1. How can I get to the Good Stuff Games Store?
   You go that way. Then make a turn and keep on going until you see the yellow sign.

2. It seems like when I even try and be with her or just fool around and stuff she always sort of tries to make it so that I won't. Do you know what I mean?

3. I think that we should use that map for the streets that this one doesn't have. This map has the main things like the key, underground stations, and that. That one doesn't have it. Do you know what I mean?

4. When do you think we will get there?
   Well, the radio is because they have to tell you when it starts.

5. How do you make pizza?
   Well, first you get the dough and then you put this stuff on the top and then you put it in the oven to bake.

6. Am I invited to your birthday party?
   Well, actually, what I mean to say is that . . . if, well . . . it seems that I just . . . well, you know how it goes sometimes.

Stage 1: Gathering Knowledge

Student activity

Work in groups of three. Make some observations of the ideas being expressed on each of the cards. Talk together about what you see as some problems in the way these ideas are expressed.

Stage 2: Promoting Understanding

Sample debriefing questions

- What observations have you made about the statements on each of the cards?
- What observations have you made about the kinds of questions being asked?
- What observations have you made about the kinds of answers given to the questions?
- What do you see as some problems with these answers?

More challenging debriefing questions

- In your view, are the questions clear? How do you suppose they might be made more clear? What suggestions do you have for making the questions more clear?
- In your view, are the answers clear? How do you suppose each answer might be made more clear? What suggestions do you have for making each answer more clear?
- What is so hard about asking clear questions? What's your theory about that?
- What is so hard about making your answers to questions clear? What's your theory about that?

- What do you suppose are some consequences of answers to questions that are not very clear?
- Why do you suppose it is a good idea to be able to answer a question clearly? What's your theory about that?

Stage 3: Applying Knowledge

- Work with a partner. Each of you write two questions about how to get from one place to another. Try to make your questions as clear as you can. Then exchange your papers, and each of you write answers to the questions. Try to make your answers as clear as you can. Exchange papers again, and give each other feedback about how your answers might be made clearer.
- Work with a partner. Each of you ask the other how to get to a certain place that is not too far from school. Then each of you write a clear set of directions for the other to follow. Exchange papers and give each other feedback about the clarity and accuracy of the set of directions.
- Work with a partner. Talk together about what you consider to be an important need for your school. Then, working together, write a short statement describing what that need is and why you think it is important. Then exchange papers with another team of students and give each other helpful feedback to make your suggestions as clear as they can be.
- Work with a partner and discuss the following problem: Your friend is having a birthday party and you have decided that you will not go because you'd rather go to the ball game with your dad. Working together, write a short letter to your friend that tells him or her of your decision. Try to make it as clear as you can and try to say it in a way that doesn't hurt your friend's feelings.
- Work with a partner. Think about a TV program or a movie that you have both seen. Talk first about what you consider to be the important ideas in this program or film. Then, working together, write a short summary of the film or program that clearly and accurately describes the main ideas of the film or program. Exchange papers with another pair and give each other helpful feedback about how your summaries might be made clearer.

Stage 4: Reflecting and Self-Evaluating

This may be done in a whole-class discussion or as a written exercise.

- Tell about how you see yourself learning to speak and write your thoughts more clearly.
- Tell about what you consider to be the importance of speaking and writing clearly.

- Tell about the problems you had in writing clear responses to these activities. How did you deal with those problems?
- Tell about the kinds of feedback you were able to give to help others in these activities.
- Where do you think you need more help?
- Tell what you consider to be your best work in these activities.

Questions that call for the examination of the quality of students' thinking for each activity are included in Chapter 5.

ACTIVITY 7:
LISTENING—A KEY TO INTERPERSONAL COMMUNICATION
(GRADES 3–8)

Learning Goals

- To promote awareness of the need to develop listening skills to understand what is being communicated
- To promote skill in listening for general understanding and for obtaining specific information

Big Ideas

- Listening means being able to hear and to understand what is being said.
- Listening requires our careful attention to what is being said.
- Listening and understanding are very important skills in interpersonal communication.
- Good listening skills help to develop better interpersonal relationships.

Thinking Operations Included in This Activity

- Observing, comparing, interpreting, examining assumptions, suggesting hypotheses, evaluating and judging, making decisions, applying principles to new situations, creating and imagining, summarizing

Materials Needed

A collection of "discussion leaders," that is, sample dialogs, for each group, for example,

Arlo: I had a bad day at school.
Grandma: You didn't wipe your feet when you came into the house!

Bertha (on the phone to Orilla): Someone's at the door. Just keep on talking and I'll be right back.

Carlos: Uh, oh. I think I've sprained my ankle.
Patsy: That's too bad. Let's go play ball.

Emilio: I want to tell you something, George.
George: I'm in a hurry to get to Sibbold's house. Tell me later.

Charlotte: Hey, Camrose. I have to tell you . . .
Camrose: Hey, Charlotte. Listen to this.

Stage 1: Gathering Knowledge

Student activity

Work in groups of three or four. Read the discussion leaders and tell what you observe to be happening in each of the situations. Talk together and decide on what you'd like to say about each of these situations. Record your ideas.

Stage 2: Promoting Understanding

Sample debriefing questions

- What observations did you make about the first situation? How do you suppose Grandma's response makes Arlo feel? What makes you think that is true?
- What observations did you make about the second situation? How do you suppose Bertha's response makes Orilla feel? What makes you think that is true?
- What observations did you make about the third situation? How do you suppose Patsy's response makes Carlos feel? What makes you think that is true?
- What observations did you make about the fourth situation? How do you suppose George's response makes Emilio feel? What makes you think that is true?
- What observations did you make about the fifth situation? How do you suppose Camrose's interruption makes Charlotte feel? What makes you think that is true?

More challenging questions

- How does it feel when you realize that someone is not listening to you? What examples can you give from your own life that describes how that works?
- How does it feel when you are trying to tell someone something and that person interrupts you? What examples can you give from your own life that describe how that works?

- Why do you suppose it is important to be a good listener? What reasons can you give to support your ideas?
- How do you suppose good listening skills help us in building friendships? How does that work? What examples can you give?
- What gets in the way of being a good listener? What makes you think that is true?
- How does good listening help us to understand? What ideas do you have about that?

Stage 3: Applying Knowledge

- Work with a good friend. Talk together and tell how it feels when you are talking and the other person is not listening. Has this happened to you? If so, tell about the situation and tell how it made you feel.
- Work alone. Write about a time when you were feeling bad and you tried to tell someone about it but that person did not want to listen.
- Work with a partner and talk together about a time when you had something important to say and your partner interrupted. Talk about how you felt. Talk about what you would have liked your partner to say. Then, working alone, write a story about what happened.
- Work with a partner. Make a list of those friends who you think are good listeners. What does good listening include? What do they do to show you they are good listeners? Working together, write a short summary of how you can tell that a person is a good listener.
- Work alone. Write a short story that shows how to become a better listener.
- Work with a friend. Make a list of what you believe gets in the way of someone's being a good listener.

Stage 4: Reflecting and Self-Evaluating

This may be done in a whole-class discussion or as a written exercise.

- Tell about how you see yourself as a listener. What examples can you give of your listening skills?
- Tell about what you think you need to do in order to become a better listener.
- Tell about where you see yourself having trouble listening to others.
- Tell what you believe gets in the way of your being a good listener.
- Tell what you consider to be some benefits of good listening skills.
- Tell how it feels when you know someone is really listening to you.
- Tell how it feels when you know someone is not listening to you.
- How did you use the information you gathered about listening in doing the activities in Stage 3?
- What were some challenges you faced in any of this work?
- What do you consider to be your best work?
- Where do think you need more help?

Questions that call for the examination of the quality of students' thinking for each activity are included in Chapter 5.

ACTIVITY 8: THE ART OF STORYTELLING (GRADES 3–8)

Learning Goals

- To promote understanding of storytelling as an art form that teaches us a lot about ourselves and others.
- To promote recognition that stories help us to grow in our awareness of our own feelings through the understanding of others' feelings
- To promote awareness that there is a great deal of pleasure and satisfaction in hearing, telling, reading, and writing a good story

Big Ideas

- Good stories come from what you know and really care about.
- Good stories are narratives that readers will want to read.
- The details in a story make the situations more real for the reader.
- A good story requires that you organize your ideas in a way that makes the story clear to the readers.

Thinking Operations Included in This Activity

- Observing, interpreting data, summarizing, comparing, collecting and organizing data, evaluating and judging, interpreting data, imagining and creating, suggesting hypotheses

Materials Needed

A copy for each person of a short story that has a powerful narrative thrust, printed on a card or paper, such as the following:

When I close my eyes and think about when I was a small girl, the image of a nickel pops into my head. We were very poor, and a nickel was a huge amount of money to me. Every day in school, the teacher would ask who wanted to buy milk and cookies. You could get a container of milk and two cookies for a nickel. But I never had a nickel. And every day when that teacher opened that box of cookies, I could smell the chocolate and the vanilla, and I wanted milk and cookies more than anything. But I had no nickel.

One morning, my father walked me to school. He was a very big man, and he had to reach way down to hold my hand when we crossed the street. He was wearing his work clothes—gray overalls that smelled of paint. He almost never walked me to school, so this day was special.

When we got to the school door, he reached into his pocket and pulled out a nickel. "Here," he said. "Here's a nickel for you." He walked away without saying good-bye, and I looked after him, shoving the nickel deep into my pocket.

Later that morning, when the teacher opened her cookie box and the smell of chocolate and vanilla filled the room, she asked, "Who wants to buy milk and cookies today?" I pulled my nickel out of my pocket shouted out, "I do! I do!" The monitor brought a container of milk, a straw, and two chocolate cookies to my desk. I shoved them into my mouth and thought about my father in his paint-splattered overalls taking the train to work.

Stage 1: Gathering Knowledge

Student activity

Work with a partner. Read the story aloud to each other. Then, talk together about some of the following questions:

- What observations were you able to make about the little girl's feelings in this story?
- What parts of the story gives you clues to these feelings?
- Discuss your ideas with each other.
- Now, take turns telling each other a story from your own childhood. Be sure to include some of the feelings you had.
- Then, work alone. Write one or two sentences to describe what you liked about your friend's story. Write about the feelings you observed in your friend's story.
- Exchange papers with your friend. Give each other a chance to read about the things that each of you liked about each other's story.

Stage 2: Promoting Understanding

Sample debriefing questions

- What observations did you make about the little girl in the story? What does the story tell about her?
- What observations did you make about the feelings being expressed in the story? What parts of the story gave you clues to those feelings?
- What observations did you make about the details the author included in the story to make the situation more real?
- What observations did you make about the kinds of feelings that this story evoked in you? How do you suppose the author created those feelings for you? What ideas do you have about it?

More challenging questions

- Tell about the stories you told about from your own childhood. Tell about the kinds of feelings your story is about.

- What kinds of clues did you use in your story to communicate those feelings? How did you know they were successful in describing the feelings?
- How did you know your story was interesting? How could you tell?
- What kinds of details did you include in your story to make it come alive for the reader?
- How did your feedback help your friend to learn more about his or her story?

Stage 3: Applying Knowledge

- Work alone. Sit back in your seat and close your eyes. Think of those times in your life that have had special importance to you. Just let the thoughts roll around in your head and see what pops out. Then, get together with a friend and share some of the thoughts you had. Which ideas did you talk about with the most feeling? Write those ideas down on a piece of paper and put it away in your "idea box."
- Work alone. You will be choosing a story to read to a younger person—a brother or sister, a neighbor or a student in a lower grade. But before choosing your story, decide on who your audience will be. Then find out what would interest this person. Does she skate? Does he dream of going camping with his dad? Does she love horses? Now, look through the books in your classroom or in the school library for a good story. Take time to select carefully just the right story. Practice reading the story several times in front of a mirror, before you read it to your audience. After you have practiced reading the story, think about the storytelling experience. Write three things that you liked about the way you did it. Write one thing you might want to improve on.
- Work with a friend. Plan an after-school trip to a place where older people live. This might be a senior citizen's residence, a community center, or even your grandmother's house. With your friend, make arrangements to visit the place. (It's probably a good idea to write a letter or to telephone first and make a date to come. Bring a tape recorder along, if you can get one.) When you are there, introduce yourselves to one or two of the people. Start chatting with them, and soon you will find that someone is telling a story. Ask permission to record the stories. As you hear them, think about the kinds of feelings that are being expressed in these stories. When you return to school, you might want to play back some of the best stories for your classmates. Perhaps you can transcribe one story and make some illustrations for it.
- Writing a story is different from telling a story. You can say words that you can't write, but in writing you get more than one chance to tell your story. You can write your story over and over again, changing ideas; taking out boring parts; adding interesting facts; and correcting spelling, punctuation, and errors in sentence structure. All writers

do this. It's called the process of editing and making revisions. You may not want to bother doing all this for every story you write, and that's OK. But sometimes you will. You will want to do this because you will know that your story is worth working on again and again, until you get it just right for you. Usually this happens when you write something you care about and you know about. Unless you can actually say to yourself, "Yes, I do care about this topic," and, "Yes, I do know a lot about this topic," there's not much point in starting. So always question yourself this way before you start.

Now, work with a friend. Talk together and try to remember some of the most boring topics you have ever written about (What I did on my summer vacation? Aaarrrgh! My favorite fish? Bleh! Spring comes to the prairies? Ugh! Igneous rocks I have collected? Pgghhht!). Use a computer, if possible, and, working together, make a list of those topics. Now, use your computer program to put your list in order with the most boring topic at the top. Make a printout of your work and compare your lists with those of another pair of students. What are some of the similarities about the most boring topic of each pair? Try to decide what it is that makes these topics so boring. What role did feelings play in any of these topics? Discuss your ideas with each other.

- Work with a friend to compare the following two stories.

> I was in a big sailboat with my friend. It was his dad's boat and we planned to look for sharks because we had all of the stuff that you use. We got it from a store that you can buy whatever you want. When we got to the place, where we wanted to go, we got all of the stuff on the boat and went into the water first. We just swam around the bottom of the ocean and then we were looking around and we saw a big white shark.

A Grade 6 boy wrote this story. His sentences are clear. You can understand what he means. But do you really care about what he is saying? If you don't, it's probably because there's not a lot of feeling behind those words. If you are going to write a story about sharks, try to think of some feelings you do know and do care about that are related to sharks.

Here's the second story, by a Grade 6 girl:

> Once we went boating and I fell into the water and I was yelling for help. I saw a shark. It was as big as a car. It had teeth 7 inches long. I was scared.

As you compare these two stories, think about how they are they alike. How are they different? How did the Grade 6 girl change *boring* to *interesting*? What role did feelings play in each of the stories?

- Work alone. Use the topic "What I did on my summer vacation" as a starter. But this time, think about feelings. Was there a very sad time in the summer? Did you ever feel lonely? Was there a scary adventure you had? Did you get hurt? Did you miss someone very much? What made you angry? What was so exciting you could hardly stand it? Now, using a computer, if possible, write about that time, telling about the wonderful/terrible/lonely/scary/horrific/sad event— as you remember it. Make your feelings come through as you write. Working on the computer, edit and revise your story so that in its final form, it says just what you want it to say. Then make a printout, exchange papers with a friend, and tell each other what you enjoyed about each other's stories.

Stage 4: Reflecting and Self-Evaluating

This may be done in whole-class discussion or as a written exercise.

- Tell what you have begun to understand about the art of storytelling.
- How, in your understanding, do feelings make stories more interesting?
- What do you suppose makes a story boring? What do you suppose makes a story interesting? What are some differences that explain it?
- What have you begun to understand about how to construct a good story?
- What challenges have you faced in your work as a judge of others' stories? How did you deal with those challenges?
- Where do you think you need more help?
- What do you see as your best work in these activities?

Questions that call for the examination of the quality of students' thinking for each activity are included in Chapter 5.

ACTIVITY 9: ASKING GOOD QUESTIONS (GRADES 3–8)

Learning Goals

- To develop skills in learning to ask good questions
- To promote appreciation for the role of questions in obtaining good information

Big Ideas

- Asking good questions is an important key to finding out what you want to know.
- Not all questions are good questions. There are important differences in the ways questions are constructed and how they are expressed.

Thinking Operations Included in This Activity

- Observing, comparing, classifying, examining assumptions, suggesting hypotheses, evaluating and judging, making decisions, summarizing

Materials Needed

Some of the following pairs of questions on cards to serve as discussion leaders.

1. Who wrote the Harry Potter books?
   What accounts for the enormous popularity of the Harry Potter books?
2. What were the names of Columbus's three ships?
   What do you know about each of Columbus's ships?
3. What is the date that the Declaration of Independence was signed?
   What was the significance of the Declaration of Independence?
4. Where are the Andes located?
   How does the geography of the Andes bear on the climate and the living conditions in South America?
5. What are the names of three characters in the story?
   Which of the characters in the story would you choose for a friend, and what criteria have you used in making your choice?

Stage 1: Gathering Knowledge

Student activity

Work in groups of four. Make some observations of the pair of questions on each card. Talk together about what you observe in each question. Then talk about what you see as the important differences in the questions. Write a short summary of your observations.

Stage 2: Promoting Understanding

Sample debriefing questions

- What observations did you make about the first question on each of the cards?
- What observations did you make about the second question on each of the cards?
- What do you see as some important differences between the pairs of questions?

More challenging debriefing questions

- What happens in your mind when you are asked the first question on the card? How do you know?

- What happens in your mind when you are asked the second question on the card? How do you know?
- What are some differences in what happens in your mind when asked the first and second questions?
- Which questions make you think more? How do you know that is true?
- Which questions help you get better information? How do you know that is true?

Stage 3: Applying Knowledge

- Work with a partner to prepare a list of questions that you will use to interview the principal of the school. Decide first what you want to find out about his or her job. Then write your list of questions so that each question gives you the kind of information you are looking for. Use the second questions on the cards as examples of the kinds of questions to be asked.
- Work with a partner. Use the Internet to find out what you can about the mayor of your town or city. Then, working together, write a list of questions to ask the mayor about what he or she plans to do about the homeless people in your town. Make sure your list of questions follows the style of the second question on each of the cards. Exchange your lists of questions with another pair of students and give each other feedback about how to improve the questions on your list.
- Work with a partner. Write a list of five questions that would require some hard thinking on a science or social studies test. Exchange your list of questions with another pair of students and give each other feedback about how to improve your questions.
- Work with a partner. Write a list of questions that you would use to interview your favorite TV or movie star. Decide first on what you want to know. Make sure you construct your questions so that none of them can be answered with either a yes or no or with a one-word answer.

Stage 4: Reflecting and Self-Evaluating

This may be done in whole-class discussion or as a written exercise.

- Tell about what you have learned about the art of asking questions.
- Tell about what you have learned about the differences between good and not-so-good questions.
- Tell about your growing understanding of how good questions make a person think harder.
- Tell about some of the challenges you faced in creating good questions. How did you face those challenges?
- Where do you think you need more help?

Questions that call for the examination of the quality of students' thinking for each activity are included in Chapter 5.

ACTIVITY 10: CREATING DRAMA (GRADES K–8)

Learning Goals

- To promote dramatic expression of all kinds, with movement and speech in harmony
- To develop an appreciation of drama as means of expressing thoughts and feelings, as well as to entertain

Big Ideas

- Drama includes verbal production as well as pantomime, charades, dance drama, and any other use of the body to imitate action and symbolize feeling.
- Drama is an important medium for expressing thoughts and feelings.

Thinking Operations Included in This Activity

- Observing, creating and imagining, comparing, evaluating and judging, making decisions, designing investigations, suggesting hypotheses, summarizing

Materials Needed

- A variety of props, for example, hats, shawls, shoes, sweaters, jackets, canes, umbrellas, aprons, baby carriage, capes, ties, cushions, dolls, fans, glasses, gloves, handbags, jewelry, mirrors, stuffed animals, suitcases, telephone, uniforms, wallets, masks, housekeeping equipment, cooking and baking equipment, music-making equipment, camera, microphone, makeup boxes, puppets, video recorder

Stage 1: Gathering Knowledge

Student activity

Work in groups of six. Use the materials to create a dramatic presentation that you will show to the rest of the class. You can dramatize any event you wish—but you need to decide together what you will do. Plan first, and then rehearse before you present your drama to the rest of the class.

Stage 2: Promoting Understanding

Sample debriefing questions

- What observations did you make about the way your group went about preparing for the dramatic presentation?
- What observations did you make about the props that were available?

- In what ways did the props contribute to the plan of the drama?
- What observations did you make about the use of speech in the drama?
- What observations did you make about the use of body movement in the drama?
- What observations did you make about the use of facial expressions in the drama?
- What observations did you make about voice intonation in the drama?
- What observations did you make about the presentation to the class?

More challenging questions

- How did you go about preparing for the presentation to the class? What observations did you make about how that was done?
- How do props enrich and enliven a drama? What are your ideas about that?
- How does the use of speech enrich the drama? What are your ideas?
- How do body movements contribute to the dramatic presentation? What are your ideas?
- How do facial expressions contribute to the dramatic presentation? What are your ideas?
- How do you know your dramatic presentation was any good? What criteria are you using to make that judgment?
- What's entertaining about drama? Why do we enjoy it? What are your ideas?

Stage 3: Applying Knowledge

- Work with a small group of friends and prepare a dramatic presentation that is done only in pantomime. You can use props, facial expressions, and body movements, but no speech. Plan what you are going to do first, and then give your presentation to the class. After your presentation, get feedback from your classmates about your presentation.
- Work with two teams of players and play several games of charades, acting out titles of books, famous quotations, names of famous people, titles of movies, or titles of TV programs.
- Work with a small group of players and select a piece of music that will serve as a background to a dramatic presentation that is done with puppets or marionettes. Plan the presentation first, and then build a puppet stage for your presentation. Get feedback from your classmates to find out how the music helped the dramatic presentation.
- Use the Internet to find out what scenes from plays you can view. Work with a friend to make some observations about the players, the props, the facial expressions, the dialogue, and the body language—all of what the actors use to get their meaning across. Write a short summary of your observations.

- Select a dramatic TV program that you like. Make some observations about how the actors play their roles, the props that are used, the facial expressions, the dialogue, the music, the body language. Write a short summary of your observations of this TV dramatic presentation.
- Work with a friend and write a script for a short radio program about any topic of your choice. Before you begin your script, it's a good idea to gather some information about how scripts are written and also about how sound effects are used in radio presentations. Because radio is an auditory rather than visual medium, you will have to figure out ways to present your story without the use of any visual images.
- Work with a friend and watch some of the YouTube dramatic presentations on the Internet. Make some observations of how these presentations are done. What scripts are used? What is the dialogue like? What props? What facial expressions? Are these presentations any good? How do you know that?
- Work with a small group of players and plan and prepare a dramatic presentation that you will eventually videotape or make a DVD of, for a class presentation.

Stage 4: Reflecting and Self-Evaluating

This may be done in whole-class discussion or as a written exercise.

- Tell about what you have come to understand about drama.
- Tell about your understanding of how facial expressions, body language, props, and dialogue contribute to dramatic presentations.
- Tell about your understanding of how drama entertains.
- Tell about some of the dramatic presentations you did and how they turned out. What was good about them? What might have been changed?
- Tell about some of the challenges you faced in the problem-solving activities in Stage 3. How did you deal with those challenges?
- What do you do best? Where do you think you need more help?

Questions that call for the examination of the quality of students' thinking for each activity are included in Chapter 5.

ACTIVITY 11:
GIVING EVALUATIVE FEEDBACK: IS IT GOOD? (GRADES 4–8)

Learning Goals

- To promote awareness of the importance of standards and criteria in evaluative feedback on written work

- To develop appreciation of the differences between helpful, nonhelpful, and hurtful evaluative feedback in written work

Big Ideas

- Helpful evaluative feedback is based upon specific criteria that allow us to decide what is good in written work.
- Evaluative feedback is a useful tool in improving a piece of written work.
- Evaluative feedback can be helpful, nonhelpful, or hurtful to the person being evaluated.

Thinking Operations Included in This Activity

- Observing, comparing, collecting and organizing data, suggesting hypotheses, evaluating and judging, interpreting data, making decisions, classifying, examining assumptions, designing investigations

Materials needed

A collection of discussion leaders on individual index cards that demonstrate different evaluative comments, such as

- You are not trying.
- You are a terrible speller.
- Your writing is poor.
- Your story is not interesting.
- It's good.
- A for your story.
- What I liked best about your story was the humor in it.
- I liked the way you began your story. It grabbed my attention immediately.
- Your writing is very clear and well organized. I can see that you had a plan and developed your ideas around that plan.
- Your use of metaphor made the story come alive for me.
- You presented the characters so clearly I felt that I knew them.
- You don't know how to use quotation marks.

Stage 1: Gathering Knowledge

Student activity

Work in groups of three or four. Make some observations of the evaluative comments on each of the cards. What observations have you made about the comments that you consider to be helpful? What observations have you made about the comments that you consider to be less than helpful? What observations have you made about the comments that you consider to be hurtful? Talk together about your observations of helpful, nonhelpful, and hurtful evaluation.

Stage 2: Promoting Understanding

Sample debriefing questions

- What observations have you made about helpful evaluative comments?
- What observations have you made about comments that are less-than-helpful?
- What observations have you made about comments that are hurtful?
- What do you see as some differences between helpful and hurtful comments?
- How would you classify these comments?

More challenging debriefing questions

- What do you see as a distinguishing characteristic of hurtful evaluation? What makes you think that is true?
- What do you see as a distinguishing characteristic of less-than-helpful evaluation? What makes you think that is true?
- What do you see as a distinguishing characteristic of helpful evaluation? What makes you think that is true?
- What's evaluation for? What's your theory about that?
- How do clear standards help in giving evaluative feedback? How, in your view, does this work?
- What are some differences between grades and evaluative feedback? What are your ideas about that?
- How do you see evaluative feedback as helpful to you in your written work? What's your idea about that?

Stage 3: Applying Knowledge

- Work with a partner. Collect some schoolwork that you have done and that has been evaluated. Make some observations about the evaluative comments and classify them into groups of the following: helpful, less than helpful, and hurtful. Make sure you have some good reasons for your decisions about your classifications.
- Work with a partner. Write a list of five evaluative comments that you believe to be helpful. Write another list of five evaluative comments that you believe to be less than helpful. Write a third list of five evaluative comments that you believe to be hurtful.
- Work with a partner. Choose a book (or a movie or TV program) that you both have read or seen and together decide on some evaluative

comments that you would write to the author or director. Make sure that you are clear, before you begin writing, about the standards that you are using to construct your evaluative comments.
- Work with a partner. Observe the comments on this card and discuss how each of them might be reworded from a hurtful, or less-than-helpful, comment, to one that is helpful.
   Try harder.
   You aren't thinking!
   You have six spelling mistakes.
   B+
   Good work.
- Work with a partner. Using your own classroom experiences, identify as many helpful evaluative comments as you can that have been significant in furthering your understanding of how to do better next time.

Stage 4: Reflecting and Self-Evaluating

This may be done in whole-class discussion or as a written exercise.

- Tell about your growing understanding of the different kinds of evaluative comments that are used in and outside school.
- Tell about your understanding of the effects of these different forms of feedback.
- Tell about your understanding of the importance of using standards and criteria as a basis for evaluation.
- Tell about your understanding of how helpful evaluative feedback contributes to your growing understanding and skill in written work.
- What were some challenges you faced in doing these activities? How did you meet those challenges?
- Tell about where you think you need more help.
- Tell what you think you have done best in these activities.

Questions that call for the examination of the quality of students' thinking for each activity are included in Chapter 5.

ACTIVITY 12:
THE LANGUAGE OF PERSUASION (GRADES 3–8)

Learning Goals

- To promote awareness of how persuasion techniques in print and on the radio, TV, and the Internet affect the way we think and feel
- To develop more sensitivity to the words and language of persuasion

Big Ideas

- Print, radio, TV, and Internet ads can affect our opinions, attitudes, and behavior.
- Commercials are designed to influence what we like and what we buy.
- Commercials and other persuasive devices (editorials, campaign speeches, slogans, name-calling) have the power to persuade us by implying that certain values, lifestyles, and behavior are better than others.

Thinking Operations Included in This Activity

- Observing, comparing, interpreting data, collecting and organizing data, examining assumptions, suggesting hypotheses, evaluating and judging, designing investigations, making decisions, imagining and creating, classifying, summarizing

Materials Needed

Several discussion leaders on cards, based on the following types of examples:

> If you want to be supercool get yourself a pair of Shortstop running shoes. It's the shoe of the stars! They give you that extra spring! Be the first one on your block with Shortstop! Super cool, dude!

> For kids who hate their vegetables, get some Blue Rose frozen peas. You can't beat their farm-fresh flavor and their home-cooked taste. Look at Billy! He never ate his vegetables before. And now he just cleans his plate. Yummmy! Hey, Mom, can I have some more Blue Rose peas?

Stage 1: Gathering Knowledge

Student activity

Work in groups of four. Make some observations of these commercials that try to persuade you to buy their products. What observations can you make about them? What words in each of them are more persuasive? Which words hook you into wanting to buy that product? What are your ideas?

Talk together about other commercials you have seen on TV or in print that make you believe that you just can't live without that product. Talk together about how those commercials do that.

Stage 2: Promoting Understanding

Sample debriefing questions

- What observations did you make about the two examples of commercials?

- What observations did you make about the particular words that are used to persuade you to buy?
- What do you see as some differences between the words with strong power to persuade and those words that are more subtle persuaders?

More challenging debriefing questions

- What examples can you give of commercials on TV or in print that urge you to buy their product? What, in your view, gives them such power to persuade you to buy?
- In what other places do you find messages that urge you to buy, or to think a certain way, or to behave a certain way? What examples can you give of such messages?
- In your view, which students are more easily persuaded? What makes you think that is true?
- In your view, which students are less easily persuaded? What makes you think that is true?
- Why do you suppose it's a good idea to be aware of the power of certain commercial messages to influence our thinking? What's the benefit of being more aware?
- Why do you suppose it's a problem for people to be easily persuaded by messages that try to influence their thinking? What's the problem with that?
- Where do you see examples of persuasion tactics in the school yard? In the classroom? At home? What examples can you give?
- How in your view do TV and print commercials affect our lifestyles? What's your idea about it?
- What do you see as the role of persuasion tactics in election campaigns? What's your theory about that?

Stage 3: Applying Knowledge

- Work with a partner. Design a poster that attempts to persuade the students in your class to vote for a particular person for class president.
- Work with a partner. Survey some newspapers and magazines and clip out those advertisements that you observe to be highly persuasive for children and teens. Talk together about what makes them so persuasive. Paste them into a scrapbook in the order in which you think they belong, from most persuasive to least persuasive.
- Work with two partners. Spend 2 hours watching television and make a list of all the commercials you have seen during those 2 hours. Which ones were the most persuasive? Which the least? Make some observations about which ones had more power to persuade.
- Work with two partners. Spend an hour studying advertisements on the Internet. Make a list of all those advertisements you have seen

during that hour. Which ones were the most persuasive? How did the ads intrude on the information? Make some observations about how ads are used on the Internet.

- Work with a partner. Design a television commercial to persuade an audience to buy a particular dog food. Use the techniques you learned about to make your commercial as persuasive as possible.
- Work with two partners. Use any resources you have to make a list of those words that have more power to persuade. Classify the words on your list and give each category a title.
- Work with a partner. Make some observations of what you have purchased in the past month or 2 that you have been persuaded to buy by print, TV, or Internet commercials.
- Work with a partner and gather some information about how persuasion tactics are used in the school yard. Write a brief summary of your findings.
- Work with a partner on the following question: Does buying a certain shirt or pair of running shoes or anything really do what the TV announcer says it will do for you? How do you explain our willingness to buy these products, even when we know that the commercial we have heard is far from the truth? How do you explain it? Write a summary of your ideas on the subject.
- Work with a partner. Use the Internet to study some blogs and, working together, make some observations of how the blogs are used to try to persuade you of a point of view.

Stage 4: Reflecting and Self-Evaluating

This may be done in a whole-class discussion or as a written exercise.

- Tell about your growing understanding of how print, TV, and Internet commercials attempt to persuade us to buy certain products.
- Tell about your understanding of the kinds of words that are supercharged to persuade us to buy.
- Tell about your understanding of how commercials affect our behavior, our attitudes, and our opinions.
- Tell about your understanding of how name-calling in school is a form of persuasion.
- Where do you think you need more help?
- On what activities did you do your best work? How do you know that is true?

Questions that call for the examination of the quality of students' thinking for each activity are included in Chapter 5.

CHAPTER 9

Building Habits of Thinking in Social Studies

History, Government, Politics, Economics, Geography, and Socially Responsible Behavior

The activities in this chapter use a teaching-for-thinking framework to examine important issues in history, government, politics, geography, and economics. This framework allows students to expand their knowledge as well as advance their understanding of critical social issues.

ACTIVITY 1: STUDYING COMMUNITIES (GRADES K–3)

Learning Goals

- To promote deeper awareness of the diversity of the communities in which people live, especially with regard to homes, population, and transportation
- To develop understanding of the many elements that make up a community
- To build appreciation and respect for individual differences within and outside the community
- To promote awareness that healthy communities are built on individuals' ability to get along with each other

Big Ideas

- Communities are shaped by the people who live in them. Communities also shape people.
- Many elements characterize a community. These include houses and other buildings, transportation, recreation, green space, and the people who live there.
- There is great variety in the ingredients that make up communities.

Thinking Operations Included in This Activity

- Observing, comparing, classifying, collecting and organizing data, examining assumptions, suggesting hypotheses, evaluating and judging, making decisions, imagining and creating

Stage 1: Gathering Knowledge

Student activity

Take a walk around your community. Walk with a partner and make some observations about the houses, factories, stores, and office buildings. Make some observations about the recreational facilities and the green space. Make some observations about the people you see. When you return to the classroom, work with your partner and draw some pictures of the buildings, recreation facilities, green space, and people in your community.

Stage 2: Promoting Understanding

Sample debriefing questions

- What observations did you make about the houses?
- What observations did you make about the office buildings? How would you describe them?
- What observations did you make about the shops? How would you describe them?
- How are the houses similar? How are they different?
- What did you observe about the people in your community?
- What did you observe about recreational facilities and green space?

More challenging debriefing questions

- How would you describe the buildings in your community? Their shapes? sizes? colors? How do you know that's true?
- Who, do you suppose, decides about the design of a building? What makes you think that is true?
- How would you describe the green space in your community? Who do you suppose decides about the green space? What makes you think that is true?
- How would you describe the kind of recreation facilities available in your community? Who do you suppose uses these facilities? What are your ideas?
- How would you describe the people in your community? What makes you think that is true?
- What role do people play in your community? What do people do that contributes to the health and safety of a community? What, in your view, do people do to weaken the health and safety of a community? What are your theories about that?

- What other communities do you know about? What do you know about them? How are they different from yours? How are they alike?
- What makes up a community? What are your ideas about that?

Stage 3: Applying Knowledge

- Whole-class activity: the designing and planning of a large mural that highlights the key elements of the community in which the children live.
- Work with a partner. Create a story about how people get from home to work in your community.
- Work with a partner and develop a list of words that are good descriptors of your community.
- Work with a partner and write a story about neighbors who did not get along together. Draw some pictures to illustrate your story.
- Work with a partner and examine illustrations of other communities, for example, communities on mountaintops, communities near the beach, communities in farming areas, communities in the suburbs, communities in a large city. How are these communities like your own? How are they different?
- Work with a partner and examine illustrations of communities in other cultures, for example, Plains Indians communities, Inuit communities, Mayan Indian communities, early American settler communities. Make some observations about how these communities are like your own and how they are different.
- Make some observations of the kinds of signs you see in your community. Work with a partner and make some illustrations of the most important signs.
- Work on your own. Study your own home and see if you can figure out what it is made of. Then draw some pictures of the way you think it was constructed.
- Work with a partner and draw a map of your community. Try to include the main streets as well as the areas you think are important.
- Work with a partner, and interview a grandparent or other relative to find out about the homes they lived in years ago when they were younger. Make some illustrations of those homes, based on what you have learned.

Stage 4: Reflecting and Self-Evaluating

It is suggested that this activity be done in whole-class or small-group discussion.

- Tell how you see yourself becoming a more thoughtful observer.
- Tell about your growing understanding of what makes a community.
- Tell about your growing understanding of the role people play in a community.

- Tell about your growing understanding of how communities are alike and how they are different.
- Tell about where you think you needed more help in doing these activities.
- Tell about what you think you did best.

Questions that call for the examination of the quality of students' thinking for each activity are included in Chapter 5.

ACTIVITY 2:
GETTING AROUND—STUDYING TRANSPORTATION (GRADES K–4)

Learning Goals

- To promote awareness of how transportation is used to move goods and people from place to place
- To further understanding of different methods of transportation and how they are used
- To elevate awareness of transportation's dependence on fossil fuels

Big Ideas

- Transportation offers ways of moving people and goods from place to place.
- Through various means of transportation, we are able to go to more places and get there faster.
- Current methods of transportation have many benefits for people; but they also increase our dependence on fossil fuels, which pollute the environment.

Thinking Operations Included in This Activity

- Observing, comparing, designing investigations, collecting and organizing data, classifying, examining assumptions, suggesting hypotheses, evaluating and judging, making decisions, imagining and creating, summarizing

Materials Needed

- For each working group: an assortment of photos or illustrations of rush hour on the freeway, cars in a traffic jam, trucks at a weighing station or truck stop, airplanes stacked up for takeoff, bicycles being used for commuting or transportation, subway trains, elevated trains, metro liners, cargo ships being loaded and unloaded, garbage trucks, oil tankers, cruise ships

Stage 1: Gathering Knowledge

Student activity

Work in groups of four. Make some observations of these different ways of transporting people and goods. What observations can you make about the cars? the trucks? the trains? the airplanes? the bicycles? the ships? Talk about what you think are the best way for people to get from place to place. Draw some pictures that show what you think is the best way for goods and people to be transported from place to place. Give each of your pictures a title.

Stage 2: Promoting Understanding

Sample debriefing questions

- What observations have you made about the way we use cars to get from place to place?
- What observations have you made about the way trucks are used to move goods?
- What observations have you made about the different kinds of transportation used to move people and goods around the world?
- What observations have you made about the needs we have for moving people and goods from place to place?

More challenging debriefing questions

- Which types of transportation are best for moving people from place to place? What makes you think that is true?
- Which types of transportation are best for moving goods from place to place? What makes you think that is true?
- How do you suppose people moved around before there were cars, trucks, trains and airplanes? What were some disadvantages of those types of transportation? What are your ideas about that?
- What do you consider to be some disadvantages of the types of transportation we use today to move people and goods from place to place? What are your ideas about that?
- How do you suppose transportation is likely to change in the next 50 years? What are your ideas about that?

Stage 3: Applying Knowledge

- Work with a partner. Make a list of all the kinds of transportation you can think of that are used to transport people around the world. Then classify the items by putting them into groups. Give each group a name.
- Work with a partner. Write a story about a bicycle and a truck that were in a race.
- Work with two partners. Go to the local supermarket and interview the manager to find out how the market disposes of its garbage. Draw some illustrations or write a short summary of what you have found.

- Work with a group of four and design a mural that shows the different types of vehicles that come through your town or city.
- Work with a partner and design a poster to try to persuade people to do more walking and bicycle riding to reduce the use of gasoline.
- Work with a partner and interview the manager of your local market. Find out what you can about where the foods and other market items come from. Create a graph to show the different kinds of foods and other market items and how far each has to travel to get to your market.
- Work with a partner and interview at least three adults. Find out how far each has to travel each day to get to work and back home again and what means of transportation each of them uses. Create a graph to show what you have found about miles traveled and means of transportation.
- Work with a group of four and design a mural to show how transportation systems have evolved over the past 100 years.

Stage 4: Reflecting and Self-Evaluating

It is suggested that this activity be done in whole-class or small-group discussion.

- What observations have you made about the different types of transportation used to move goods and people from place to place?
- What observations have you made about the different kinds of vehicles used in transporting people and goods?
- What observations have you made about how garbage is transported?
- What observations have you made about how transportation systems have evolved over the past 100 years?
- What observations have you made about the use of fossil fuels in our systems of transportation?
- What were some challenges for you in this unit of work?
- Tell where you think you did your best work.

Questions that call for the examination of the quality of students' thinking for each activity are included in Chapter 5.

ACTIVITY 3: JOBS AND WORK (GRADES 3–8)

Learning Goals

- To promote understanding of the different kinds of jobs and work that people do to make communities and societies function
- To promote appreciation for the different kinds of jobs people do that help us in various ways
- To develop understanding that work is the process through which people earn money, which allows them to buy the things they need

Big Ideas

- People work at different kinds of jobs.
- Different jobs require different talents, skills, and abilities.
- People work to earn money, which allows them to buy the things they need.
- The work that people do and the money they earn for that work is not directly related to the significance of the job.

Thinking Operations Included in This Activity

- Observing, comparing, classifying, problem solving, imagining and creating, suggesting hypotheses, examining assumptions, collecting and organizing data, evaluating and judging, making decisions, designing investigations, summarizing

Materials Needed

- For each working group: a photograph of Shaquille O'Neal side by side with a photo of a teacher, captioned: "Shaquille O'Neal earns $31 million a year; Ms. Jones, a Grade 4 teacher, earns $45,000 a year."

Stage 1: Gathering Knowledge

Student activity

Work in groups of four. Observe the photos of these two workers. Shaquille O'Neal is a famous basketball star. Ms. Jones is a wonderful Grade 4 teacher. How are the jobs of these two workers different? What observations can you make about their work?

Stage 2: Promoting Understanding

Sample debriefing questions

- What observations have you made about Shaquille O'Neal's work?
- What observations have you made about Ms. Jones's work?
- How are their jobs alike? How are they different?
- What kind of talent or skill does one need to become a teacher? A basketball player? What makes you think that's true?

More challenging debriefing questions

- What is hard about being a basketball player? What are your ideas?
- What is hard about being a teacher? What are your ideas?
- How do you account for the difference in salary of these two workers? What hypotheses can you suggest that would explain such differences?

- How much should a teacher get paid for his or her work? What are your ideas?
- How much should a basketball player get paid for his or her work? What are your ideas?
- What's so important about being a basketball player? How does that work help us?
- What's so important about being a teacher? How does that work help us?
- What other kinds of jobs do people do that make important contributions to our lives? What are your ideas about that?

Stage 3: Applying Knowledge

- Work with a group of four. Make a survey of all the kinds of jobs that mothers/fathers/grandparents/caregivers do among the students in the class. Design a mural that shows the different kinds of jobs and work that are found among the families of the students in the class.
- Work with a partner. Study the list below that shows how much money Shaquille O'Neal spends in 1 month on his living expenses (from www.mediatakeout.com.2008/2123).
  - $156,116 to pay for the mortgages on three homes
  - $31,299 in homeowners insurance
  - $3,345 in phone bills
  - $1,610 in lawn and pool maintenance
  - $12,775 in food
  - $1,495 in cable TV
  - $24,300 in gas
  - $6,730 in dry cleaning
  - $17,220 in clothing
  - $2,305 for pets
  - $110,505 for vacations

  Make up a comparable budget for what you think Ms. Jones's expenses are for 1 month.
- Work with a partner and write a story about what it might be like to work in a restaurant. Be prepared to read your story to the other students in the class.
- Work with a partner. Try to imagine what it is like to work in the field of moviemaking. Draw some pictures and write a story about your work in movie making.
- Work with a group of four. Make a list of every kind of job you can think of. Then classify the list of jobs and give each group a name.
- Work with a partner. Begin with a discussion of the kind of work that needs to be done in and around your school. What kinds of jobs need to be done? Who are the workers? Who is there every day? Who comes in and out of the school from different places to perform jobs? How would you describe all this work? Write a short summary to describe the kinds of work that go into running a school.

- Work with a group of four. Begin with a discussion of unusual types of jobs, such as deep-sea diver, archeologist, tugboat captain, forest ranger, subway sweeper, scientist, veterinarian, lion tamer, circus clown, circus acrobat, undercover police officer, musician, orthodontist, pilot, newspaper reporter. Draw some pictures to create a collage that shows the different kinds of work done by these people.
- Work with a partner and do an Internet search on the kinds of work that can be done by people with different physical challenges. Begin with a discussion of how people rise above their physical challenges to perform important work. Write a summary of your findings.
- Work with a partner and talk to some adults in your family to find out how people lose their jobs and what some consequences are for their families. Write a story and draw some illustrations to show what you have learned.
- Work with a partner and interview grandparents to find out the kinds of work they did or do now. Write some stories about those jobs.

Stage 4: Reflecting and Self-Evaluating

This may be done in a whole-class or small-group discussion.

- What observations have you made about different kinds of jobs and work that people do in and outside our communities?
- What observations have you made about the salaries of people who do different kinds of jobs?
- What have you begun to understand about the differences in salaries of these workers?
- What have you begun to understand about how the work that people do makes a difference to our lives?
- What have you begun to understand about how salaries from jobs enable us to buy the things we need to live?
- Where did you find your greatest challenges in these activities?
- Where do you think you did your best work?

Questions that call for the examination of the quality of students' thinking for each activity are included in Chapter 5.

ACTIVITY 4: SOCIAL RESPONSIBILITIES (GRADES K–8)

Learning Goals

- To promote awareness of the need for developing social skills that help people get along with each other
- To develop awareness of the need to respect others and their feelings
- To promote awareness of the need for more socially responsible interpersonal behavior among people in the global community

Big Ideas

- The beginning of socially responsible behavior lies in the way people talk to and act toward each other. What you say to others and how you treat them can make them feel good or bad.
- Socially responsible behaviors include sharing, taking turns, cooperating, respecting the ideas of others, developing friendships, and learning from others.
- Everyone is responsible for playing his or her important part in developing positive relations with other individuals and groups.

Thinking Operations Included in This Activity

- Observing, comparing, classifying, suggesting hypotheses, creating and imagining, evaluating and judging, making decisions, examining assumptions, designing investigations

Materials Needed

- For each working group: a selection of photographs of children in arguments—in classrooms, in school, or on the school yard—with evidence of much heatedness and potentially aggressive behavior; photos of adults in arguments; photo of a war scene (armed forces, tanks, battleground, and so on)

Stage 1: Gathering Knowledge

Student activity

Work in groups of four. Make some observations of the photographs. What do you see happening in each? What do you see in the photograph that allows you to make those statements?

Talk together about how you think arguments start. How come people get into arguments? What examples can you give from your own experiences about how arguments start? and about how arguments often end?

Then talk about how grown-ups get into arguments. How are grown-ups' arguments like children's arguments? How are they different?

Now, talk about how countries get into arguments. How are the arguments between countries like children's arguments? How are they different? What do you see as some consequences of the arguments between countries?

Stage 2: Promoting Understanding

Sample debriefing questions

- What observations have you made about the photographs showing children in arguments?

- What do you observe in the photographs that tells you about the behavior of each of the children?
- What examples can you give of your own experiences in arguments?
- What observations have you made about the differences between grown-ups' and children's arguments?
- What observations have you made about the differences between arguments between countries and arguments between children?

More challenging debriefing questions

- How do arguments start? What theories do you have about that?
- How do arguments get out of hand? What theories do you have about that?
- What do you see as some potential consequences of arguments between children? Between adults? Between countries?
- How do you suppose arguments can be prevented? What theories do you have about that?
- Why do you suppose it's important to try to prevent arguments? What theories do you have about that?
- How does rude and inappropriate behavior and language contribute to arguments? What theories do you have about that?
- What do you see as each person's role in trying to avoid getting into really bad arguments? What ideas do you have about that?

Stage 3: Applying Knowledge

- Work with a partner. Try to think of as many words or phrases as you can that you have heard on the playground that are kind as well as those that are unkind. Classify these words into groups and give each group a name.
- Work with a partner. Talk together about the role of competitive sports in promoting more cooperative or less cooperative behaviors. Give some examples of both kinds of situations. Draw some pictures that illustrate your ideas.
- Work alone. Try to remember the kindest thing another student ever did for you. Remember how that made you feel. Now try to remember the kindest thing you ever did for another student. Write a short story about kindness to others and others being kind to you.
- Peter and David had a bad argument. And now, they are not speaking to each other. You are a friend of both Peter and David. How do you think you can help them to regain their friendship? What might you do? Work with a partner and try to figure out a plan.
- Maria is walking down the street and some children begin to call her names. You and your friend see this happening. What do you do? Work with a partner and try to figure out a plan. What would you say to the children who were teasing Maria? How might they react? Write your ideas.

- Sharonna's dog died. She was feeling very sad and was unable to get her work done. You and your friend want to help her to feel better. What might you do? What might you say? Work with a partner and try to figure out a plan. How do you think she might react? Talk about a time when you felt very sad and a friend helped you to feel better. Write a story about it.
- Sonja is a new girl in your class. English is a new language for her, so she has a lot of trouble with her reading and writing assignments. Some children make fun of how she talks and the different clothes she wears. Work with a partner and try to develop a plan that would make Sonja feel more welcome in your class. Develop another plan that would address the way some classmates make fun of her. Write your ideas.
- When some countries or groups of people cannot resolve their arguments, they sometimes go to war. Work with a partner, and use the Internet to find out what you can about war, how it starts, how countries get involved, and what the consequences are for all people.
- Intolerance—the holding of grudges against a group of people for their beliefs, their color, their ethnic background, their religion, or their nationality—causes people to act cruelly to others. Sometimes, the result of intolerance is just bad behavior. Sometimes, it results in more cruel acts of violence, mayhem, and murder. Work with a group of four and find out what you can about situations in the United States, for example, where intolerance has resulted in violence against people and groups. Use the library or the Internet to gather your information. Work together to find out what you can about how such intolerance grows. Write some stories about what you have found out.

Stage 4: Reflecting and Self-Evaluating

This may be done in a whole-class discussion or as a written exercise.

- What observations have you made about how arguments develop and grow?
- What observations have you made about how arguments can be avoided?
- What observations have you made about the role of language in leading to arguments?
- What observations have you made about the differences in arguments among children, adults, and countries?
- What observations have you made about where some arguments lead?
- Tell about your growing understanding of the role that each of us plays in furthering or learning to avoid arguments.
- Tell about your growing understanding of what "socially responsible" behavior is.

Questions that call for the examination of the quality of students' thinking for each activity are included in Chapter 5.

ACTIVITY 5:
STUDYING ANCIENT CIVILIZATIONS:
ANCIENT EGYPT (GRADES 4–8)

Learning Goals

- To promote awareness of an ancient civilization that developed and flourished in the Middle East beginning around 2000 BC and lasting until around AD 400.
- To further understanding of how farming allowed formerly nomadic people to settle in one place.
- To promote awareness of the rise of governments to establish order and control the population

Big Ideas

- The ancient Egyptians formed the first nation 5,000 years ago; their civilization lasted for almost 3,000 years.
- Their advanced skills in farming, crafts, and trade allowed their civilization to flourish.
- With the growth of cities, governments were needed to establish rules and to control the population.

Thinking Operations Included in the Activity

- Observing, comparing, classifying, summarizing, collecting and organizing data, examining assumptions, suggesting hypotheses, evaluating and judging, designing investigations, making decisions, imaging and creating, interpreting data

Materials Needed

- For each working group: Any illustrations from textbooks, library books, or the Internet that show images of this ancient Egyptian civilization may be used to accompany the short narrative below. (See especially http://images.google.ca/ images?hl=en&q=Ancient+Egypt+-+images&um=1&ie=UTF-8&sa=X&oi=image_result_group&resnum=1&ct=title)

  Pharaoh was the name given to the kings of ancient Egypt. Pharaohs were rich beyond your wildest dreams and the people believed that they were gods. In this ancient society, the pharaoh was at the head of the government. Pharaohs made the rules and laws and had absolute control over the entire civilization.

The Nile River was essential to the rise of ancient Egyptian civilization. It created the rich, fertile soil that was perfect for farming. Food was plentiful, and there was a great variety of foods available. Once the people had the skills to farm and raise their own food, they no longer needed to wander the land in search of food to keep themselves alive.

The Nile was also a water highway. People could travel by boat to other, nearby cities to trade goods. The Egyptians' ability to use wind as a means of powering a ship was a brilliant technological advance. This led the way to later sea travel.

Besides being able to farm and grow their own food, ancient Egyptians were skilled craftsworkers, building their own homes and making their own pottery, jewelry, and clothing. They also had the skills to build the most fantastic structures, such as the Pyramids, which are still standing.

The ancient Egyptians were one of the first peoples to write things down. They wrote by using little pictures as symbols, called hieroglyphics, on a form of paper called papyrus. The ability to read and write made an enormous difference to the society. A written alphabet, the basis of reading and writing, and a system of numbers allowed this civilization to take a major step forward.

This ancient civilization lasted for almost 3,000 years!

Stage 1: Gathering Knowledge

Student activity

Work in groups of four. Read the very short story about ancient Egypt and study the pictures. Talk together about the observations you have made from the story and from the pictures about this ancient civilization.

Stage 2: Promoting Understanding

Sample debriefing questions

- What observations did you make about this ancient civilization?
- What observations did you make about the importance of farming in ancient Egypt?
- What observations did you make about the government of ancient Egypt?
- What observations did you make about their talents and skills?
- What observations did you make about their technology?

More challenging debriefing questions

- What do you suppose contributed to the rise of this civilization in the Nile Valley? What are your ideas?
- How do you suppose farming contributed to the end of nomadic life? What are your ideas about that?
- Why do you suppose that people who live in large groups require rules and laws to govern their behavior? What are your theories about that?
- What do you see as some limitations to a government that is ruled by a single, powerful figure, such as a pharaoh? What are your ideas?
- How do you suppose these ancient Egyptians developed the skills they needed to build structures such as the Pyramids? What are your ideas about that?
- Why do you suppose trade was important? What theories do you have about that?
- How, in your view, does a written-down numbering system and alphabet contribute to a society? What changes does it bring? What are your theories about that?

Stage 3: Applying Knowledge

- Work with a partner and, together, create a time line to show the development of the ancient Egyptian civilization.
- Work with a partner and study a piece of hieroglyphic writing and its translation. See if you can make sense of what the symbols represent.
- Work with a partner and, using any materials you choose, make a model of a pyramid.
- Work with a partner and search the Internet to find out what you can about the building of the Pyramids. Write a short summary and draw some illustrations that show how these structures were built.
- Work with a partner and use the library or the Internet to find out about what pharaohs had buried in their Pyramid tombs. Draw some pictures of the kinds of things that were buried with the pharaohs.
- Work with a partner and use the library or the Internet to find out what you can about mummification. Working together, draw some illustrations to show the process of mummification.

Stage 4: Reflecting and Self-Evaluating

This may be done in whole-class discussion or as a written exercise.

- Tell about your growing understanding of the ancient civilization of Egypt.
- Tell about your growing understanding of how farming enabled the ancient Egyptians to remain in one place.
- Tell about your growing understanding of the need for rules and laws for people living in large groups.

- Tell about your growing understanding of the importance of the Nile River to this civilization.
- Tell about your growing understanding of the importance of a written alphabet and a system of numerals to this civilization.
- What were some challenges you faced in these activities? How did you deal with them?
- Where did you do your best work?

Questions that call for the examination of the quality of students' thinking for each activity are included in Chapter 5.

ACTIVITY 6:
STUDYING THE BILL OF RIGHTS (GRADES 4–8)

Learning Goals

- To promote familiarity with the explicit content of the Bill of Rights amendments to the U.S. Constitution
- To promote understanding of the meanings of the amendments with respect to the laws of the United States

Big Ideas

- The Bill of Rights is the name given to the first 10 amendments to the U.S. Constitution.
- The Bill of Rights limits the powers of the federal government and protects the rights of all citizens, residents, and visitors in U.S. Territory.
- The Bill of Rights protects the freedoms of speech, press, and religion; the right to keep and bear arms; the freedom of assembly; and the freedom to petition and prohibits unreasonable search and seizure, cruel and unusual punishment, and compelled self-incrimination.

Thinking Operations Included in This Activity

- Observing, comparing, summarizing, examining assumptions, suggesting hypotheses, evaluating and judging, interpreting data, making decisions, imagining and creating, designing investigations, collecting and organizing data

Materials Needed

- A copy of the Bill of Rights—a duplicate of the original document, if possible. See, for example, the primary document from the Library of Congress: http://memory.loc.gov/cgi-bin/ ampage?collId=llsl&fileName=001/llsl001.db&recNum=144

Stage 1: Gathering Knowledge

Student activity

Work in groups of four. Working together, make some observations of this copy of the Bill of Rights. Talk together and discuss your observations of these 10 amendments to the U.S. Constitution and what you think each one means.

Stage 2: Promoting Understanding

Sample debriefing questions

- What observations have you made about Amendment 1? 2? (and so on).
- What observations have you made about a citizen's rights that are protected by the bill?
- What observations have you made about the limitations placed on the federal government by the bill?

More challenging debriefing questions:

- How, in your view, does the bill protect you and your family? What are your ideas about that?
- What's an amendment? Why do you suppose the Constitution needed these amendments? What's your theory about that?
- How does the bill establish the laws of the land? How does this work? What's your theory about that?
- Why do you suppose a citizen's rights had to be protected in this way in the early days of the country? What hypotheses explain this need?
- Why do you suppose the role of the federal government had to be limited? What hypotheses explain this need?
- What's so important about the Bill of Rights? What's your theory about that?

Stage 3: Applying Knowledge

- Work with a group of six divided into three pairs. Each pair selects two amendments and makes a poster for each that illuminates how it protects your rights.
- Work with a partner. Summarize each of the amendments in the bill.
- Work with a partner. Interview two adults and find out what they know about the Bill of Rights. Write a short summary of your findings.
- Work with a partner. Use the library or the Internet to find out what you can about freedom of the press and why such freedom is important in a democratic society. Write a short summary of your findings.
- Work with a partner. Talk together about what additional amendment you'd like to see included in the Bill of Rights. Write your amendment and give a reason for its inclusion in the Constitution.

Stage 4: Reflecting and Self-Evaluating

This may be done in whole-class discussion or as a written exercise.

- Tell about the kind of information you gathered about the Bill of Rights.
- Tell about your growing understanding of the meaning of the amendments.
- Tell about your growing understanding of why the bill was needed.
- Tell about your growing understanding of how the bill protects our rights as citizens.
- What were some challenges you faced in these activities? How did you deal with them? Where do you think you did your best work?

Questions that call for the examination of the quality of students' thinking for each activity are included in Chapter 5.

ACTIVITY 7:
THE TRIAL OF SOCRATES—JUSTICE AND LAW IN ANCIENT GREECE
(GRADES 5–8)

Learning Goals

- To give students an opportunity to examine the pros and cons in making judgments about some important issues in the trial of Socrates
- To raise awareness about the ambiguities in examining data and drawing conclusions

Big Ideas

- There are many sides to an argument, and often there is no clear right or wrong.
- People see events through their own personal biases.
- Preaching ideas that are far removed from the norm can get a person in a lot of trouble.
- What is considered radical changes with the times and with our evolving values.

Thinking Operations Included in This Activity

- Observing, comparing, interpreting data, examining assumptions, making decisions, applying principles to new situations, suggesting hypotheses, collecting and organizing data, designing investigations

Materials Needed

- The "Case of Socrates," below, may be duplicated and distributed to working groups. The case may be supplemented by any appropriate illustration; see, for example, *The Death of Socrates*, by Jacques-Louis David, at http://www.bc.edu/bc_org/avp/cas/his/CoreArt/art/neocl_dav_soc.html

    In Athens, in 399 BC, Socrates, philosopher and teacher, was tried and convicted of corrupting youth. He was sentenced to death. After a month in prison, he was given a cup of hemlock to drink in execution of his sentence.

The case of Socrates is presented in two opposing points of view. One is by Plato, Socrates' student, who lived to carry on his teacher's work. The other is by Ameipsias, a dramatist who was a contemporary of Socrates and who wrote plays in which Socrates' ideas were ridiculed.

Notes from Plato's Diary:

My teacher was a great man. What his countrymen did to him was a terrible injustice. Only a corrupt democracy like ours in Athens could do such a wicked thing. I hope that I will be able to clear his name and set the record straight.

His teaching was more concerned with helping his students learn to think rather than to follow obediently the teachings of their parents. He wanted his students to learn to question, to be critical, and to be rational in their actions. I realize that in teaching these radical ideas, he was calling for revolutionary change in the way students are educated. As a civilized people, we must be open to change, open to progress, and open to developing the minds of our youth. We cannot expect civilization to make advances if youth are not allowed to think and if they must follow blindly in the footsteps of their fathers.

Do teachers who advance new ideas and social change deserve to die? What is wrong with a society that does this?

Notes from Ameipsias's Diary

There is no question that Socrates was a very influential teacher who had a great impact on his students. We must be very careful of such teachers. Through their radical ideas, they attack the very fundamental structure of our society.

After all, it has been our tradition since the time of Homer that a school-age boy receive his advanced education at home from the elders in his family. Socrates wanted this to be changed. He wanted education to take place in universities, with professional teachers, where students would learn to criticize and challenge the teaching of their parents.

Socrates was inviting youthful rebellion and disobedience to parents. He was guilty of infecting the new generation with his ideas. It is for fathers and elders to transmit ideas to the young—not a curriculum taught in schools. Socrates was a dangerous teacher, and he had to be silenced lest he continue to corrupt the youth of this society.

Stage 1: Gathering Knowledge

Student activity

Work in groups of six and together, read the "Case of Socrates," as presented in the diaries of Plato and Ameipsias. Talk together about the two different points of view about this famous Greek philosopher and teacher and then discuss the study questions below.

- What, in your view, were Plato's strongest arguments in favor of what Socrates did?
- What, in your view, were Amiepsias's strongest arguments against Socrates?
- Where do you stand with respect to these opposing views about this teacher?

Stage 2: Promoting Understanding

Sample debriefing questions

- What do you know about the society in Athens in which Socrates lived in 399 BC? Where did your ideas come from?
- Based on your observations, how would you describe Socrates' teaching?
- What observations have you made about Plato's argument in favor of Socrates?
- What observations have you made about Amiepsias's arguments against Socrates?
- What do you see as the significant differences between the two views?
- Where do you stand with respect to these two views?

More challenging debriefing questions

- Socrates took many risks in his teaching, by advancing ideas that were new, different, and radical for his times. Should teachers advance radical ideas? What are your thoughts on this?
- Do you know of other examples of great men and women who took great risks in advancing new ideas? Who, in your opinion, are these people? How have we benefited from their ideas?
- What do you know about Greek society in the 2nd century BC? Where did your data come from? How do your data help you to understand the trial and punishment of Socrates?
- The ancient Greeks prided themselves on their love of learning. They loved studying; they loved to debate important issues and hungered to know more. How do you explain what happened to Socrates in relation to this ethos?
- To what contemporary issues does the "Case of Socrates" relate? What are your thoughts about it?

Stage 3: Applying Knowledge

- Work with a small group and, together, write a dramatic sketch and act out the trial of Socrates. Be prepared to present your play to the class.
- Work with two partners and make a large mural of a scene in Athens during the time of Socrates.
- Work with three partners and do some library or Internet research

to find out what you can about the contributions to modern society
made by the ancient Greeks in the arts, theater, architecture, music,
education, philosophy, and sports. Write a short summary of the
contributions of the Greeks in each of these fields.
- Work with a partner and draw a time line that shows the significant
  events that occurred in ancient Greece, from 1450 BC to the fall of
  the empire around 323 BC.

Stage 4: Reflecting and Self-Evaluating

This may be done in whole-class discussion or as a written exercise.

- What knowledge have you gathered about the ancient Greeks?
  Where did you get your information? How do you know it's true?
- What have you grown to understand about the trial of Socrates?
- What have you grown to understand about the risks involved in
  presenting new and radical ideas to a society?
- What have you grown to understand about the lessons this case
  teaches us?
- Tell where you faced some challenges in this work. How did you
  deal with them?
- Tell about where you think you did your best work.

Questions that call for examination of the quality of students' thinking for
each activity are included in Chapter 5.

ACTIVITY 8: SEARCHING FOR HISTORY IN ART (GRADES 4–8)

Learning Goals

- To appreciate the role of art in furthering historical understanding
- To promote understanding that art may represent lives and times
  of the past and that what is illustrated is shaped by the eye of the
  artist, not by historical truth

Big Ideas

- Artists living in earlier times have left their work to represent images
  of the lives and times of those early periods.
- While we can draw much information from these works of art about
  the history of a period, what is represented is always subject to the
  bias in the eye of the artist.

Thinking Operations Included in This Activity

- Observing, comparing, collecting and organizing data, examining
  assumptions, suggesting hypotheses, evaluating and judging,
  designing investigations, making decisions, interpreting data,
  imagining and creating, summarizing

Materials Needed

- A collection of images of works of art from various historical periods. Student groups should have at least six images to study. They can be from different eras or different images from the same era depending on how this study meshes with the overall instructional plan. Art books, school texts, and the Internet should provide for an extensive variety of images, to include paintings, sculpture, cave art, jewelry, masks, and photographs. See, for example,
  - *Bruegel:* http://www.ibiblio.org/wm/paint/auth/bruegel/dance.jpg
  - *Terra-Cotta Warriors:* http://images.google.ca/images?hl= en&q=terra+cotta+warriors++images&um=1&ie=UTF- 8&sa=X&oi=image_result_group&resnum=1&ct=title
  - *African Masks:* http://images.google.ca/images?hl=en&q= african+masks++images&um=1&ie=UTF-8&sa=X&oi=image_ result_group&resnum=1&ct=title
  - *American Indian Art:* http://images.google.ca/images?um=1&hl= en&q=american+indian+art&btnG=Search+Images
  - *Washington Crossing the Delaware:* http://www.metmuseum. org/explore/gw/el_gw_bigimage.htm

Stage 1: Gathering Knowledge

Student activity

Work in groups of four. Study the illustrations of works of art that illustrate historical events. What observations can you make about the art itself? What observations can you make about the historical era or event that this work of art represents? Talk together about your observations.

Stage 2: Promoting Understanding

Sample debriefing questions

- What observations have you made about the art? About the materials used to produce the art?
- What observations have you made about the way the artist uses design, color, light and dark, form, and perspective to illustrate the event or period of time?
- What observations have you made about the historical period or event in which the particular piece of art was produced?
- What can you tell for sure about the period or event? How do you know that is true?
- What can you tell about the people who lived during these times? How do you know that is true?
- What observations can you make about the artist? What assumptions have you made?

More challenging questions

- What can you tell about the different ways in which artists illustrated their lives and times?

- What's the difference between an artist's illustration of an event and the actual event? What are your ideas about that?
- Many people in many different cultures use different forms of art to represent the lives and times of the people in those cultures. Why do you suppose art is important to a culture? What are your ideas about it?
- How does the art of a period help in our understanding of that historical period? What are your thoughts about it?
- How is the art of these historic periods different from and similar to the art of today? What examples can you give of those similarities and differences?

Stage 3: Applying Knowledge

- Work with a partner. Make some illustrations, using any medium of your choice, of what you consider to be an important current event, to give people in the future an idea of what our lives are like today.
- Work with a small group to design and illustrate a large mural depicting the life and times of young people in your community today.
- Work with two partners. Use the Internet to make some observations of the terra-cotta warriors: http://images.google.ca/images?hl=en&q=terra+cotta+warriors++images&um=1&ie=UTF8&sa=X&oi=image_result_group&resnum=1&ct=title. Write a summary of what these figures tell you about the time in which they were made.
- Work with two partners. Use the library or the Internet to examine some illustrations of the lives of American Indians. What do the illustrations tell you about the culture and ways of life of these peoples? Write a summary of what you have observed about their lives.
- Work with a partner. Use the library or the Internet to examine some illustrations that were made during the American Civil War. What do the illustrations tell you about the culture and this historical time? Write a summary of what you have observed about these times.
- Work with a partner. Use the library or the Internet to examine some illustrations of the slave trade. What do these illustrations tell you about the trade in African human beings? Write a summary of what you have observed about this trade.

Stage 4: Reflecting and Self-Evaluating

This may be done in whole-class discussion or as a written exercise.

- Tell about your growing understanding of how artists tell about the times in which they lived, through their works of art.
- Tell about your growing understanding of the differences between what is represented in artistic images and that which is historical truth.
- What were some challenges for you in these activities? How did you deal with them?
- Where do you think you did your best work?

Questions that call for the examination of the quality of students' thinking for each activity are included in Chapter 5.

ACTIVITY 9: STUDYING RACISM (GRADES 3–8)

Learning Goals

- To promote awareness of the many forms of racism and intolerance toward individuals and groups
- To further understanding of the roots of racism and intolerance
- To develop appreciation for the role of each individual in taking a stand against racism and intolerance

Big Ideas

- Racism makes it possible for people to behave in ways that they would otherwise consider irrational, inhuman, and evil.
- Identifying a particular individual or group as undesirable allows us to treat them in less than human ways.
- Racial hatred is responsible for terrible injustices, for violence and murder against individuals and groups.
- Racism comes from irrational fears about others. These fears may be exaggerated by public officials in times of societal stress.

Thinking Operations Included in This Activity

- Observing, comparing, summarizing, collecting and organizing data, examining assumptions, suggesting hypotheses, evaluating and judging, designing investigations, making decisions, imagining and creating, interpreting data, classifying

Materials Needed

- Norman Rockwell's illustration of Ruby Bridges being accompanied to school on the first day of desegregation in the South along with the short paragraph about the illustration. See, for example: http://en.wikipedia.org/wiki/File:The-problem-we-all-live-with-norman-rockwell.jpg

Stage 1: Gathering Knowledge

Student activity

This is an artist's painting of a real event that occurred in Louisiana, on November 14, 1960. Ruby Bridges is 5 years old. She is going to her 1st day in kindergarten. But she has to have four federal marshals walk with her—for fear of her life. You see, in New Orleans, this is the 1st day that Black children were allowed to enter what had been all-White schools—the 1st day of desegregation of the schools in the South. Make some observations of the painting and talk about the kinds of racist behaviors that you believe would lead to the need for such protection of this 5-year-old girl.

Stage 2: Promoting Understanding

Sample debriefing questions

- What observations have you made about the painting? What ideas was the painter, Normal Rockwell, trying to get across? What are your ideas about that?
- What might Ruby Bridges be feeling at this time? What is there in the painting that would lead you to believe that? What assumptions are you making?
- Why do you suppose the federal marshals' faces are not shown in the painting? What hypotheses can you suggest to explain it?
- What do you suppose might have happened to Ruby if she had not had this protection on her walk to school? What makes you think that is true? What assumptions are you making?
- What do you know about the results of desegregation of the schools in the American South in 1960? Where did those ideas come from? What assumptions are you making?

More challenging debriefing questions

- What do you know about the segregated schools down South? Where did your ideas come from? What assumptions are you making?
- Why do you suppose it was necessary for federal marshals to walk to school with Ruby? What kinds of behaviors were they trying to prevent? What are your ideas?
- What do you suppose people were afraid of with respect to Ruby's coming to her new school? What are your ideas about that?
- Why do you suppose it was so hard to desegregate the schools? What theories do you have about that?
- How come good people behave in racist ways? How do you explain it? What are your theories about it?
- What other examples can you give, from history, of individuals and groups of people who were subject to extreme forms of racist behaviors? Where do your ideas come from?
- What examples can you give from your own experiences that are evidence of racism or of discrimination of any kind? What do you consider to be the reasons for those racist behaviors?
- What do you see as an individual's responsibility in the face of racist behaviors? What assumptions are being made?

Stage 3: Applying Knowledge

- Work with a partner. Use the library or the Internet to find out what you can about Martin Luther King Jr. And his role in the desegregation of the South. Write a summary of what you have discovered.

- Work with a partner. Use the library or the Internet to find out what you can about apartheid in South Africa. Talk together and write a comparison of how apartheid was similar to and different from segregation in the American South.
- Work with a partner. Use the library or the Internet to find out what you can about the imprisonment of Japanese Americans during World War II. Interview some Japanese Americans to learn more about their own family's history during this time. Study some of the cartoons from newspapers and magazines that instilled racial hatred against the Japanese. Write a summary of what you have discovered about these events.
- Work with a partner. Use the library or the Internet to find out what you can about the Holocaust during World War II. Collect photographs and other images that you can put together in a collage to show the brutality, violence, and murder of the Jews during this time.
- Work with a partner. Interview some adults to find out what their personal experiences have been with racism, discrimination, and intolerance. Working together, write a short story that illuminates these events.
- Work with two other students. Use the library and the Internet to discover how feelings about Muslims have changed in the United States since September 11, 2001. Write a short summary of what you have discovered.
- Work with two other students. Use the library or the Internet to discover what you can about the treatment of American Indians after the settlement of the American West. Draw some illustrations to show what you have learned.
- Work with a partner. Make a list of all the words and phrases you can think of that reveal discriminatory feelings against another person or group. Then, working together, classify the words on your list and give each group a name.

Stage 4: Reflecting and Self-Evaluating

This may be done in whole-class discussion or as a written exercise.

- Tell about your growing understanding of the term *racism* and the kinds of behaviors that are racist.
- Tell about your growing understanding of where racist behavior comes from.
- Tell about your growing understanding of the many forms of racist behavior.
- Tell about your growing understanding of why some people would want to treat others as less desirable.
- Where have you done your best work on these activities?
- Where did you face some challenges? How did you deal with them?

Questions that call for the examination of the quality of students' thinking for each activity are included in Chapter 5.

ACTIVITY 10: STUDYING COMMUNICATION (GRADES 3–8)

Learning Goals

- To promote understanding of the various ways and means people use technology to communicate with each other—for better or for worse
- To promote awareness of how advanced technology makes instant communication possible across the world and the benefits and disadvantages of that

Big Ideas

- We communicate with others to express our ideas and feelings, to get our questions answered, and to send messages of little and great importance.
- Communication can be carried out in several ways—through speaking, writing, illustrations, images, and body language.
- Technology has enabled us to communicate more quickly and across greater distances using a variety of advanced communication tools, such as cell phones, fax machines, E-mail, television, radio, text messaging, and devices that capture and transmit images.

Thinking Operations Included in This Activity

- Observing, comparing, classifying, summarizing, collecting and organizing data, examining assumptions, suggesting hypotheses, evaluating and judging, designing investigations, making decisions, imagining and creating

Materials Needed

- A collection of photos or illustrations of various communication devices, for example, handset telephones, cell phones, computers, television sets, radios, newspapers, and magazines

Stage 1: Gathering Knowledge

Student activity

Work in groups of four. Make some observations of the different communication devices that are seen in these illustrations. What observations can you make about each? What observations can you make about how each is used to communicate ideas or news about events? What observations can you make about which are better to use to communicate the news? to send a message to a friend? to tell your grandmother you are coming to visit? to invite your friends to a birthday party? to tell a story?

Working together, write a brief description of each communication device and describe what kind of communication it is best used for.

Stage 2: Promoting Understanding

Sample debriefing questions

- What observations have you made about each of these communication devices?
- What observations have you made about how each is used to communicate to others?
- What observations have you made about what kind of communication each is best used for?
- How could you compare these devices; for example, how are newspapers and cell phones different? What are your ideas?
- What observations have you made about the advantages of each of these devices in communicating ideas?
- What observations have you made about the limitations of each of these devices in communicating ideas?

More challenging debriefing questions

- Why do you suppose we need so many different ways of communicating to others? What do you see as some advantages to all these devices? What are your ideas?
- What's so important about being able to communicate quickly to each other? What makes you think that is true?
- How did people manage to communicate with each other 100 years ago, before there were cell phones and computers and E-mail? How do you suppose they got their messages through? What are your ideas?
- How are images used to communicate ideas? How does this work? What are your ideas about that?
- What do you see as some drawbacks to all these high-tech communication devices? What are your ideas about that?
- More and more people are seen in the streets using cell phones to talk to each other. What do you suppose they might be saying that is so very important?
- How are radios and television sets useful in communicating ideas? newspapers? magazines? What are your ideas about that?

Stage 3: Applying Knowledge

- Work with a partner, and draw some illustrations that communicate ideas to people without using language.
- Work with a partner, and make a survey of everyone in the class to find out who uses the following communication devices: cell phones,

fax machines, E-mail, letter writing, text messages, transmitting images. Draw a graph to show the extent of usage of these devices.
- Work with a partner and make a survey of who uses cell phones and the kinds of messages they transmit on their phones. What types of messages are most frequently sent? Design a chart to show the extent of usage of cell phones and the kinds of messages children most frequently send on these devices.
- Work with two classmates and, together, try to imagine a world without telephones, computers, or other high-tech communication devices. Write a story about a boy and girl who needed to send some important messages and didn't have high-tech tools to use.
- Work with two classmates and invent a communication device that you think we might be using 50 years from now. Draw some illustrations of this device and describe the kinds of messages that will be sent with it.
- When Paul Revere needed to deliver the message that the British were coming, at the beginning of the American Revolution, he got on his horse and rode from town to town, shouting his message to all the residents. In that way, he alerted the colonists to be on guard and to be prepared for the invasion of the British. Work with a partner and talk together about how a cell phone might have helped Paul Revere to communicate this message. How would a cell phone have made a difference? Draw some illustrations to show the differences between these two ways of communicating the message.
- Work with a small group of friends and, together, choose a story that deals with some issue of social significance that you will act out as a television program. Be prepared to present this to your class.
- Work with a partner and, together, write a newspaper account of some event that occurred at your school or in your neighborhood. Make sure you communicate the news about the event clearly, so that readers will understand what happened and how.
- Work with a partner and talk about how people communicate with animals and how animals communicate with people. Draw some illustrations to show how this communication works.

Stage 4: Reflecting and Self-Evaluating

This may be done in whole-class discussion or as a written exercise.

- Tell about your growing understanding of the various ways in which people use technology to communicate with each other.
- Tell about your growing understanding of the advantages and disadvantages of these communication devices.
- Tell about your understanding of the different forms of communication that humans use.
- Tell about your growing understanding of how communication devices allow us to communicate faster and over greater distances.
- Tell about where you think you did your best work.
- Tell about where you think you need more help.

Questions that call for the examination of the quality of students' thinking for each activity are included in Chapter 5.

ACTIVITY 11:
STUDYING GEOGRAPHY—READING AND MAKING MAPS
(GRADES 3–8)

Learning Goals

- To promote awareness of how maps are constructed, their key symbols, and how they are read and interpreted
- To further skill development in the reading and making of maps
- To promote appreciation for the uses of maps in locating places in the world

Big Ideas

- Maps are symbolic representations of geographical places.
- Map reading enables us to determine distance between places and helps us to locate places in the neighborhood, the community, the state, the nation, and other countries; find recreational areas, resources, seaports, bodies of water, mountain ranges, and centers of population.

Thinking Operations Included in This Activity

- Observing, comparing, collecting and organizing data, examining assumptions, summarizing, suggesting hypotheses, evaluating and judging, designing investigations, interpreting data, making decisions, imagining and creating

Materials Needed

- For each working group: a road map of the community in which the students live. Preferably a large scale map. Good-quality road maps can be obtained from local AAA offices or from nearby gas stations. Note that the map selected for study should be one that the students can read easily and not beyond their level of maturity.

Stage 1: Gathering Knowledge

Student activity

Work in groups of four or five. Study the map showing the area in which you live and make some observations of what you see. What observations can you make about the streets in your community? What observations can you make about distances from place to place? What observations can you make about the colors used? What observations can you make about parks? recreational areas?

bodies of water? mountain ranges? centers of population? What observations can you make about the symbols used in the map? What other observations can you make? Talk together and then write a summary of your observations.

Stage 2: Promoting Understanding

Sample debriefing questions

- What observations have you made about this map?
- What has the map told you about streets in your town? About distances? About the parks? About the recreational areas? About bodies of water? About mountain ranges?
- What observations have you made about the symbols used in the map? How did you figure out what the symbols meant? How do you know that is true?
- What observations have you made about how the map tells you about distance? What does the legend at the bottom of the map tell you about how to interpret distances? How do you know that is true?
- What observations have you made about the boundaries of the map? What observations have you made about the size of the area covered by the map? How do you know that is true?

More challenging debriefing questions

- How does the map tell you about east and west and about north and south? How do you know that is true?
- How can you figure out how to get from one place to another using the map? Give an example to show how that is done.
- How can you figure out the distance from place to place using the map? Give an example of how that is done.
- What do you consider to be some important uses of maps? How do maps help us? What are your ideas?
- What other kinds of maps do you know about? How are they different from and similar to this map here?
- How are maps different from globes? How are they similar?
- How are maps made? What are your ideas about that?
- How do you know if a map is accurate? How can you figure that out?
- What did you figure out about the symbols used in the map? How do the symbols help you to interpret what is found in the area? What are your ideas?

Stage 3: Applying Knowledge

- Work with a partner and study the information on a globe of the world. What observations can you make about the information in a globe? Working together, write a short summary of the information you found.
- Work with a partner and find a world atlas in the library. Use the atlas to locate a map of the United States. Use the symbols in the atlas to help you find the major landforms, for example, the plains,

plateaus, mountains, rivers, lakes, and oceans. Working together, create a map of your own state, and highlight the landforms you have found in the map in the atlas.

- Work with two classmates. Go to the library to find some road maps of the United States. Use the maps to figure out the shortest distance between
  - New York and San Francisco
  - Chicago and Dallas
  - Gainesville, Florida, and Albuquerque, New Mexico
  - Los Angeles and Chattanooga, Tennessee
  - Newark, New Jersey, and Denver, Colorado
  - Nome, Alaska, and Santa Fe, New Mexico

  Do some double-checking to make sure your calculations of distance are as accurate as they can be.

- Work with a partner and make some observations of a map of the United States or Canada. See how many capitals of states or provinces you can find. Make a list of as many capitals as you can.

- Work with two classmates and make some observations of a map of Europe. What mountain ranges can you identify? What does the map tell you about the tallest mountain ranges and the highest mountains? Record your data.

- Work with a partner. Study a map of the southwestern United States and see what you can observe about the rivers in this part of the country. What does this study of rivers tell you about the land in this part of the country? Record your information in a short summary statement.

- Work with a partner and sign on to the Internet to locate MapQuest. Use MapQuest to determine how to get from the street where you live to Disneyland, in California. Summarize your findings in a short statement that highlights the best way to travel.

- Work with a partner and imagine what it was like for Lewis and Clark, the two explorers who mapped the Oregon Trail, to make the first maps of the Pacific Northwest. Write a story describing those events.

- Work with a partner. Use the library or the Internet to find out about Global Positioning Systems (GPS). How does GPS work? What uses does GPS have? Work together and write a summary of your findings.

Stage 4: Reflecting and Self-Evaluating

This can be done in whole-class discussion or as a written exercise.

- Tell about your growing understanding of the uses of maps.
- Tell about what you have discovered about the symbols in maps and how they are used to locate specific places.
- Tell about your growing understanding of how maps are used to determine distance between places.
- What were some challenges you faced when doing these activities?
- Where have you done your best work?

Questions that call for the examination of the quality of students' thinking for each activity are included in Chapter 5.

ACTIVITY 12:
STUDYING EARLY HUMAN BEINGS—WE ARE ALL RELATED
(GRADES 3–8)

Learning Goals

- To promote awareness about our earliest ancestors, who appeared on the earth about 5 million years ago
- To further appreciation that although we do not look alike today, we have all come from the same ancestors
- To promote appreciation for the quality of life of early humans, their habitations, and how they dispersed across the world
- To raise awareness of the controversies that underlie the study of evolution and the interpretation of data from these early sources

Big Ideas

- While humans today do not look at all alike, we are all descended from one small group of people—the earliest humans.
- While new data continue to emerge about our where our earliest ancestors lived, we do know that they dispersed, over many thousands of years, throughout the world.
- Early humans lived in small groups, like tribes. They hunted and gathered their food. They had to keep moving in search of new sources of food for survival.
- They used animal skins to make clothing and eventually learned to use fire to keep warm and to cook food.
- Controversy continues about the theory of evolution, in spite of considerable evidence to support the theory.

Thinking Operations Included in This Activity

- Observing, comparing, summarizing, collecting and organizing data, examining assumptions, suggesting hypotheses, evaluating and judging, designing investigations, classifying, summarizing, interpreting data, imagining and creating, making decisions

Materials Needed

- At least six illustrations of early humans found in school texts, and especially library books with visual images of prehistoric lives and times; include, especially, a map showing where earliest humans originated and their routes across the continents (see, for example, Grant, 2000; Thomas, 1995; Vialou, 1996).

Stage 1: Gathering Knowledge

Student activity

Work in groups of four. Study the illustrations of the lives and habitats of these early humans. Make some observations of their appearance, their clothing, their tools, the land in which they lived, and the ways in which they got their food. Make some observations of the maps that show how the tribes spread throughout the world. Be prepared to share your ideas in the debriefing.

Stage 2: Promoting Understanding

Sample debriefing questions

- How would you describe the appearance of these earliest humans?
- What observations have you made about their clothing? the ways in which they got their food? the way the people in the tribe worked together? their habitats?
- What observations have you made about the routes they traveled across continents?
- What observations have you made about their tools?
- What other observations have you made that allowed you to understand the kind of lives these early humans lived?

More challenging debriefing questions

- How, in your view, have humans changed over the past 5 million years, since these early humans walked the earth?
- How do you suppose they learned to make tools? to make fire? to hunt animals for food? which plants to eat? What are your theories about that? What assumptions are you making?
- How come, if we are all descendents of early humans, we now look completely different from them? What theories do you have about that? What assumptions are you making?
- How would you describe the quality of their lives? What makes you think that is true?
- How do you suppose these illustrations have been made, since there were no photographs at that time to show us how they really looked? What theories do you have about that?
- How can we tell if the information presented in these maps and illustrations are true? What assumptions are being made?
- Why do you suppose the early humans dispersed across the Earth? Why didn't they just stay in one place? What ideas do you have about that?
- Since they had no means of transportation, how on earth did they manage to travel these huge distances? What theories do you have about that?
- Since life was so hard, how do you suppose they managed to survive? What theories to you have about that?

- How do you suppose we moderns learned so much about these early humans? How do you explain it? How can we know that what we learned was accurate? What are your ideas?

Stage 3: Applying Knowledge

- Work with a partner and create a diorama showing a scene from the lives of early humans.
- Work with a partner and find out what you can about the kinds of foods that were hunted and gathered by early humans. Make a list of the foods and classify them.
- Work with two classmates and, using the library as a resource, make some drawings of your impressions of early humans that lived around 5 million years ago.
- Work with a partner and find out what you can about the animals that inhabited the earth around 5 million years ago.
- Work with a group of four or five and create a time line to show the development of early humans from 5 million years ago to the first civilizations in the Middle East.
- Work with a partner and write a short story about the journey of a tribe of early humans from one area to another, in search of food.
- Work with two classmates and find out what you can about the controversies surrounding the theory of evolution. What are some strong arguments for the theory? What are some arguments against? After you have gathered your data, present your own point of view on the theory and supply evidence for your position.
- Work with two classmates and find out what you can about how different tribes of early humans made war against each other. Write a short summary of what you have found.
- Work with two classmates and find out what you can from the library or the Internet about how archaeologists search for evidence of early humans and how they interpret the data from their digs to learn more about early human lives. Write a short summary of your findings.

Stage 4: Reflecting and Self-Evaluating

This can be done in a whole-class discussion or as a written exercise.

- Tell about your growing understanding of early humans, the quality of their lives, and how they managed to travel across the earth.
- Tell about your understanding of these early humans as our ancestors.
- Tell about what you have learned about their lives, their tribes, their clothing, their tools, and their habitats.
- Where did you face some challenges in these activities? How did you deal with them?
- Where do you see yourself having done your best work?

Questions that call for the examination of the quality of students' thinking for each activity are included in Chapter 5.

PART IV

Reflections on Practice

CHAPTER 10

Growing Teachers of Thinkers

The 6th graders were in their seats, listening politely to the teacher, who was giving them some information about school assignments. Lenny, his brow furrowed, raised his hand. "Ms. Owens," he asked, "yesterday you said that we were going to be responsible for all the examples in the math text. And today you told us that some of those math skills are not that important for us to learn. So how do you explain that inconsistency in your statements?"

What does a teacher, who has worked hard at enabling her students to become more thoughtful, more critically aware, and more discriminating, do in response to students' confrontational feedback? What kinds of personal and professional characteristics mark the teacher of thinkers and the classroom climate that encourages and supports freedom to think?

There is an ethos to a classroom in which thinking is prized and cultivated that goes beyond the teaching strategies and activities discussed in earlier chapters. This ethos comes more from the teacher's beliefs and attitudes that form his or her modus operandi, providing an openness that includes a willingness to relinquish control, comfort with uncertainty, and an absence of defensiveness in the presence of tough questions and critical feedback. While these behaviors are learned, they are also rooted in who we are and in what we consider important in the education of students.

For those experienced teachers who have already embraced the principles and practices of teaching for thinking and are seeking affirmation, encouragement, and a few new ideas, nothing that appears in these pages will be new. For those preparing to teach, and for those teachers who are seeking to "change their stuff," this chapter will identify those teacher attributes that support such a climate for thinking. For this latter group of teachers, this is likely to mean a sea change in the ways in which they perceive the role of the teacher.

RELINQUISHING CONTROL

Let me begin by confessing that during my own professional training, and throughout my first years of teaching, I believed, with unshakeable conviction, that the main job of the teacher was to establish control and to hold tight to that control, so that students would all obey, listen, and behave! I believed, deep in my heart, that children were not capable of making their own decisions about matters of consequence and that furthermore, to provide them with freedom to choose would invite mayhem. I loved the idea of being in control; it gave me a sense of security, a feeling that I was doing just what a teacher was expected to do. My program was run on a tight schedule, and classroom rules and regulations were spelled out clearly so that all children knew what was expected of them—the iron fist in the velvet glove. When children misbehaved or failed to comply with the rules and schedules, they received polite, but firm, reprimands. I was the teacher! Today, I cringe at such memories, and I am shamefaced to admit those beliefs.

It wasn't until after my 4th year of teaching that I began, slowly, to relinquish classroom controls, by allowing my Grade 3 students to make modest choices for themselves. They could choose their own books in what was my first attempt at an individualized reading program. I made these shifts in my program and in my behavior with great caution and certainly with considerable doubt about where it might all lead. Yet, to my astonishment, the children could and did choose their own reading materials, and to my further amazement, the sky did not fall. I was delighted to find that children actually benefited from being allowed to choose and that reading performance and behavior, rather than suffering, actually improved.

From these early and inauspicious beginnings, I have made huge shifts, in beliefs as well as in actions, with respect to relinquishing classroom control, whether I am teaching primary, middle grade, high school, or university students, for giving students freedom to choose has become so ingrained, and now so natural, that I couldn't conceive of doing otherwise. It is imbedded in my belief system that students need to learn to choose for themselves and that providing them with these opportunities empowers them as people and as learners. It is not enough to allow choice when the issues are inconsequential; the big step forward is in encouraging and embracing students' rights to choose in matters of significance—to have a voice in what they do.

Relinquishing control means that you, as the teacher, do not have to be in charge every moment of every school day. It means that you can listen to students who have ideas that are different from yours and respect what they have to say. It means that you don't have to be right all the time. It means that you don't have to play the guru with all the answers and can ask students for suggestions and listen to them. It means that you can be wrong and admit it frankly and freely. You can be free to be human.

Regrettably, I do not have any neatly packaged set of ideas for how teachers might begin to relinquish their needs for control over their students. I do know, however, that it can begin with an identification of that need within oneself, followed by a growing understanding of how such a need relates to a perceived sense of loss of personal power. This is a tricky mixture of personal-emotional stuff, and I believe that each of us has to sort this out in his or her own way. But I also believe that the need for personal power is a key emotional need in all of us. When that need is threatened, we tend to want to exert more control, which makes us feel safer and more secure. When our own need for personal power is adequately met, it is easier to relinquish control. That is quite a simple paradigm for a lifetime of serious self-study, for giving up behaviors that are no longer productive and replacing them with a new set of behaviors that are more in accord with creating a climate of thinking in one's classroom.

The pathway to relinquishing control is not a freeway, where you can travel at breakneck pace and get to your destination tomorrow. It requires a long, hard look at self, to determine where your starting point is and what you see as impediments to that journey. It requires the kind of self-scrutiny that allows you to know, with a degree of objectivity, about the kind of behavior you are using to control student behavior and what steps you need to take to move from those positions. It requires you to see the discrepancies between believing that you *are* allowing for choice, and actually allowing for choice. It requires you to feel safe in the process of giving up control—with certainty that you are doing what is right and good for students and for their learning.

It is impossible to have a climate for thinking in which the teacher's controls have not been relaxed. Thinking means students have the freedom to think their own thoughts, to make up their own minds, to examine alternatives, to leave questions unanswered. Without freedom to choose, students are denied their chances of growing toward independence in their problem-solving and decision-making processes. Each time the teacher chooses for students, a building block of developing that independence is lost.

No, I do not promise you a rose garden. But for myself, I can say that when I was finally able to let go of my own need for control, I felt liberated by the convincing evidence that my students were being empowered as thinkers (Wassermann, 2004).

TEACHERS AND STUDENTS AS PARTNERS IN LEARNING

It is not easy to visualize a classroom in which teachers and students are partners in the process of inquiry. Tradition puts teachers in an elevated position, if not that of physically standing on a platform, then certainly in the mental image of teacher-student relationships. The portrayal of teachers as disseminators of knowledge and of students as empty vessels has a long and venerable history and is what is most represented in documents, photographs, films, and stories about classrooms. The idea that a teacher has something, anything at all, to learn from students, is anathema to what most traditionalists think of when they picture classroom instruction. The apocryphal story about a teacher who was providing individual instruction to students while the principal was making his supervisory observation and who told her, "I'll come back when you're teaching," comes to mind (Wassermann, 1993).

Yet in a classroom where the teacher cultivates a climate for thinking, "teaching objectives shift from knowledge transference to student transformation—where qualities of mind (curiosity, judgment, and wisdom) and qualities of person (character, cooperation, and open-mindedness) become key" (Christensen, 1995, p. 7). What such transformation requires of the teacher involves some risk, for it means stepping away from the role of expert, shedding the garb of the all-knowing sage, and treading cautiously into the role of co-inquirer with students. Rather than dishing out morsels of information, teachers are asking questions; rather than declaring truths, teachers are trying to obtain the fundamental, even total, involvement of the student. It requires thinking about the student, not the subject matter, first; "when you get that involvement and bring both mind and emotion into the classroom" that's heady stuff (Christensen, 1995, p. 7).

This, of course, does not mean that teachers should not know, or need not know, the subject matter of what they are attempting to teach. But it does mean that knowing the student and working with each individual student trumps the subject matter every time. The teacher is not only a master of the content, but equally knowledgeable of the "who"—the student—and the "how"—the steering of the questioning and responding dialogue.

Such an inversion of the traditional teaching-learning paradigm is likely to mean a significant shift in style—perhaps a new you. A significant part of that new you is shedding the mantle of defensiveness that has protected all teachers throughout history from any critical question, any deviation from the norm, any suggestion that they are less than powerful in maintaining dominance over all aspects of classroom life. It means involving students in the "thinking act," not to find the right answer, but to engage in the process of inquiry, with each student's contribution seen as a precious thing, for it represents his or her efforts to think. As teachers embrace this process, their own learning—about the student, about the student's thinking, about the very process of inquiry—is enhanced.

LEARNING TO WATCH AND LISTEN TO YOURSELF TEACH

There are teachers who adhere strictly to predetermined sets of procedures and apply them regardless of the need to assess each new classroom situation thoughtfully, on its own differential terms. They often neglect to see into the heart of problems and consequently apply "wrong" or inappropriate strategies to deal with situations. When the strategy does not work, these teachers are likely to blame the students for not responding as they should have done. When confronted with the inappropriateness of their action in response to a problem, they are likely to respond defensively, unwilling to take a deeper look at how they themselves have misapplied strategies or misread the problem. Because they have not learned to watch themselves in action, these teachers have limited capability to learn from their own actions. Their teaching is an unexamined act—there is no art to what they do (Wassermann & Eggert, 1991).

Looking at oneself clearly and objectively in the act of teaching is not for the faint of heart. For enduring self-study, there is no better tool than a recording device—audio for the more cautious, video for the more intrepid. In replaying a recording, listen for the kinds of questions being asked, the amount of teacher talk, the amount of student talk. Figure 10.1 provides a tool for enabling such self-scrutiny.

When two teachers work together, this partnership can be enormously additive in contributing to skill development. Partners can provide support for each other, help examine each other's interactive style, and together make plans for further professional development.

More intensive self-study can be made if the teacher is willing to take on the very arduous task of making a verbatim transcript of at least 10 minutes of the classroom discussion and subjecting that transcript to critical analysis. While it is very tedious to transcribe everything that is being said, even in a 10-minute interval, there is great value in the minute examination of every word and question, of tone and nuance, and of the effect of each question and response on the next student statement. A guide for undertaking this critical analysis is provided in Figure 10.2.

My own first steps in this self-scrutiny were both aided and abetted by a videotape recorder. Up until that first glimpse of myself in action, I had thought that everything I was doing in the act of teaching was, in every way, contributing to the thinking of my students. I believed that what I was doing in both my curriculum work and in my discussion strategies was exemplary in carrying out this goal.

It was a hard fall to reality. Until seeing and hearing myself in action on video, I had no clear appreciation of the ways in which my questions worked to persuade my students to follow my lead in arriving at the specific answer I was looking for. Far from engaging in open inquiry, I manipulated them and subtly directed them to where I wanted them to go.

To open oneself to critical self-scrutiny asks a lot of teachers. It's much easier to deny, to avoid, to rationalize—but those are not steps to professional growth. It is very hard to accept one's faults, one's shortcomings, one's warts, and to begin from that point to work on change. No one likes to admit to flaws, and this is especially so in these modern times, when shirking fault has become a national pastime. But it is the only road to professional growth.

Figure 10.1. Recording Sheet for Analysis of Teacher Responses in Classroom Discussion

A. Responses That Inhibit Thinking
  1. *Responses that bring closure*
     Agrees with student's idea
     Doesn't give student a chance to think
     Tells student what he or she (teacher) thinks
     Talks too much/explains it his or her way
     Cuts student off
     Other closure responses
  2. *Responses that promote fear*
     Heckles/is sarcastic/puts down idea

B. Responses That Limit Student Thinking
  Looks for single, correct answer
  Leads student to "correct" answer
  Tells student what to do
  Gives information

C. Responses That Encourage Thinking
  1. *Basic responses that encourage reexamination of the idea*
     Saying the idea back to student
     Paraphrasing
     Interpreting
     Asking for more information, e.g., "Tell me a little more about that," or
         "Help me to understand what you mean"
  2. *Responses that call for analysis of the idea*
     Give me an example
     What assumptions are being made?
     Why do you suppose that is good?
     What alternatives have you considered?
     How does (that) compare with (this)?
     How might those data be classified?
     What data support your idea?
  3. *Responses that challenge*
     What hypotheses can you suggest?
     How do you interpret that?
     What criteria are you using?
     How would those principles be applied in this situation?
     What predictions can be made based on those data?
     How would you test that theory?
     What new scheme/plan can you envision for that situation?
  4. *Responses that accept a student's idea nonjudgmentally*
     I see
     Thank you

D. Responses Unrelated to Debriefing the Big Ideas
  Classroom/behavior management responses
  Speech mannerisms
  Other

Note: Adapted from Wassermann, 2004, p. 113.

For me, the hard looks I took at my own teaching opened up a world of reflection-on-action. That first step put me on the path of studying my interactions and learning to listen as I speak, a burdensome habit for any teacher. Such professional commitment means taking responsibility for every utterance that comes out of one's mouth. It means listening to every word that is spoken to others. It means carrying the burden of owning our own statements and learning to observe and apprehend how those statements are affecting others, discerning whether they are effective in producing the desired learning results. It also requires knowing something about the interactions that are helpful in promoting student thinking and learning as well as those that are counterproductive to that process.

Teaching, in this world of self-scrutiny, becomes an examined act. It allows teachers to narrow the gap between their espoused educational goals, their perceptions of what they are doing, and the reality of classroom life.

Figure 10.2. Analysis of Teaching-for-Thinking Discussion Skills

1. Describe your response pattern during the discussion. What responses were most used? least used? (e.g., saying back? paraphrasing? interpreting? analyzing? challenging?)

2. To what extent did your teaching-for-thinking interactions promote students' examination of the big ideas?

3. To what extent were you able to attend to students' ideas?

4. To what extent were you able to be respectful and nonthreatening in your responses, while at the same time working with students' ideas, helping them to examine issues of consequence?

5. What do you see as some good features of your teaching-for-thinking interactions?

6. What aspects of your interactions need more work?

7. What new insights did you acquire about discussion teaching from your work on this activity?

CHAPTER 11

Evaluating Student Progress

Every classroom teacher wants to know how well his or her students have learned the material that has been taught. And all parents are entitled to know how their children have succeeded in school. Every teacher also needs to know where and how a student is having difficulty, what the nature of the difficulty is, and what kinds of teaching strategies should be used to remediate the difficulties. The need for assessment that truly and substantively supports and furthers student learning is a critical component of classroom life.

In the quest for such information, it is easy to understand the appeal of standardized tests. They are easy to administer and easy to mark. Their claims of validity and reliability dazzle us into accepting their legitimacy, despite our knowing with some certainty that numerical representations of behavior can be faulty, misleading, or downright wrong. What's more, standardized tests are hopelessly inadequate in providing the kind of useful feedback that teachers need to make diagnoses of students' learning needs. While the No Child Left Behind law of 2001 has elevated the use of such standardized tests to be the *sine qua non* of classroom evaluation, the data coming from their 8-year use has given further evidence of their paucity as classroom assessment tools (Bracey, 1998; Kozol, 2005; Lewis, 2007). Moreover, as tools to evaluate student thinking, they are wanting in the extreme.

STANDARDS OF PERFORMANCE IN THINKING

From their own professional observations, most teachers know the extent to which a student has learned and what that student's learning needs are. This teachers know from observing and interpreting the day-to-day behavior of the student, witnessed in that student's performance on a variety of learning tasks over the course of a school year. It is in the ongoing, careful study of student behavior, written work, and interactions with peers and teacher that the essential elements of what students know and the extent to which they know it can be observed and interpreted.

Aiding the teacher in this task of assessing student behavior are the criteria or standards against which the student behavior is judged. Most teachers use their own sets of standards, as well as those issued by the school district, to communicate to parents how well their children have learned and what learning deficits need attention. This chapter builds on what teachers already do in making assessments of student learning. It identifies criteria that are related to intelligent habits of mind and provides behavioral profiles that permit comparisons between a student's day-to-day behavior and the criteria.

The standards of intelligent functioning provided in Figure 11.1 are adapted from those originally generated by a group of secondary school teachers seeking better ways to evaluate student progress in the cognitive domain. They are not subject specific, but represent an overview of what the teachers hoped to see as students became more thoughtful, more responsible, and more independent as thinkers and learners. Once the criteria were identified, these teachers went further, to design assessment tools that gave them a means of zeroing in on how students' day-to-day behaviors, on a variety of learning tasks, measured up to the criteria.

Figure 11.1. Standards of Performance in Assessing Thinking

Behavioral standards identified by teachers as descriptors of desirable qualities of intelligent functioning include the following:

Quality of Thinking
1. Sees the big ideas
2. Shows tolerance for the ideas and opinions of others
3. Shows tolerance for contrary data; is open-minded
4. Is original, inventive, creative in work

Attitudes About Thinking
5. Has a high tolerance for uncertainty, ambiguity
6. Is cautious in drawing conclusions; conclusions are based in data
7. Functions on his or her own initiative
8. Embraces thinking as a means of solving problems
9. Is open to self-evaluation; is open and nondefensive in self-evaluation

Thinking Skills
10. Gathers and organizes data intelligently
11. Gives examples in support of ideas
12. Generates hypotheses that are reasonable and are appropriate means of addressing a problem
13. Makes intelligent interpretations of data
14. Differentiates between opinion and fact, between assumption and fact
15. Makes evaluative judgments that are rooted in appropriate criteria
16. Makes thoughtful, intelligent choices with respect to problems, ethical issues, and moral dilemmas

PROFILES OF THINKING-RELATED BEHAVIOR

Because behavior is not a constant condition but a set of complex and vary-ing states of being, it is not possible to assess, with perfect accuracy, its exact nature. What can be assessed, however, are the patterns seen in the behavior: Is it more or less this than that? Is it more prevalent, or less seen? Is it acute, or subtle? Is it pervasive, or sporadic? Each of us has good days and bad days, and our behavior may shift accordingly. But in assessing behavior, what we want to know is to what extent certain behaviors are prevalent, and consistent, and how they reflect overall who the student is and how he or she responds in a va-riety of situations. The teacher who observes students' behavior every day, in a variety of contexts, is the best judge of that. It is from these observations that the wisest and most informed assessments of the extent to which the behavior represents a pattern, rather than a once-in-a-while occurrence, can be made.

The secondary school teachers who designed the assessment tools de-veloped a set of profiles—descriptions of "what a student's behavior should look like" if he or she met their criteria for intelligent functioning. The Pro-files of Student Behavior was the result of their efforts (Adam, Chambers, Fu-kui, Gluska, & Wassermann, 1991). When students showed serious, thought-ful behavior in dealing with activities, assignments, and other classroom tasks, the assessment tools bore that out. Where students were still found wanting in applying their intelligent habits of mind, the assessment tools revealed where and how more work had to be done. The standards and the assessment tools allowed teachers to use their professional judgment in eval-uating the "what" and the "how" of students' performance in the cognitive domain and generate remedial measures to address student growth needs.

One of the more helpful aspects of the profiles is that they describe be-havior in concrete terms, which allows for greater accuracy in assessment. Used as a diagnostic tool, they highlight students' competencies and weak-nesses in their thinking abilities, as well as providing a focus for writing evaluative reports and conducting parent-teacher conferences.

The Profiles of Student Behavior, originally written for secondary school students, served as a template for this chapter's new set of profiles, devel-oped for the purposes of assessing thinking-related behaviors for elementary and middle school students. Teachers are welcome and encouraged to use them to evaluate students' thinking-related behaviors in their classrooms.

EVALUATING THINKING-RELATED BEHAVIOR

Evaluating students' classroom behavior is a complex task. It is difficult for a teacher who is occupied with many teaching responsibilities to concentrate on the kinds of behavior students are exhibiting and to remember such behavioral patterns for a large number of students. To facilitate this process, it is suggested that teachers use a 4-point rating scale to provide a summary of student performance in each of the behavioral areas described in the profile, as well as to allow for a means of documenting student growth. Students can be rated as follows:

+3 if the teacher observes the behavior as present almost all of the time
+2 if the teacher observes the behavior to be in evidence often
+1 if the teacher observes the behavior to be present some of the time
-1 if the teacher observes the behavior not to be present at all, or to
be the antithesis of what is described in the profile, indicating a
substantive deficit in this particular thinking skill.

Ratings that would fall consistently on the negative side of the equation for any student would be regarded as indication that such a student's classroom functioning has failed to meet basic standards associated with intelligent habits of mind and that much, much more work in thinking is necessary to help the student develop higher order thinking skills. On the positive end of the scale, a student who receives ratings consistently at the +3 or +2 level would reveal great strength in those thinking skills that we associate with intelligent and mature functioning in a variety of curriculum tasks. Wherever possible, students themselves should be involved in the assessment process, so that they may determine, to the best of their ability, how they see themselves functioning in relation to these profiles.

Behaviors Related to Quality of Thinking

1. Sees the big ideas. These students are able to see the larger picture in the examination of topics or issues. When they present a point of view, they address the issues of substance. They are able to differentiate between what's important and what is trivial. They don't get bogged down in details. They are able to appreciate the complexity of big ideas.

2. Shows tolerance for the ideas and opinions of others. These students are open minded about ideas that are different from theirs and do not believe that their ideas alone are the right ones. While they may not agree with others' ideas, they are able to listen respectfully, see the other point of view, and consider that opinion rationally and thoughtfully. They are thoughtful, respectful, and rational in their responses.

3. Shows tolerance for contrary data; is open minded. Although these students are likely to hold strong beliefs of their own, they are open to the consideration of ideas and data that are contrary to their own. When these students examine ideas that are different, they do so thoughtfully and rationally. They are not dogmatic about what they believe and are open to listening to different opinions.

4. Is original, inventive, creative in work. These students are able to go beyond the ordinary, to create ideas. They are original and inventive, and what comes from their minds is fresh, new, and imaginative. They take risks in their creative work and push the limits of what is ordinary, in generating something new. They do not need the safety of well-established routines and formulas and are open to new ideas and innovation. Change, rather than intimidating them, is embraced.

Behaviors Related to Attitudes About Thinking

5. Has a high tolerance for uncertainty, ambiguity. These students are able to live comfortably in the land of uncertainty. They don't need to have the answer to a particularly thorny problem; they are able to suspend judgment and wait until more information is at hand. Uncertainty does not unsettle them; while it creates cognitive dissonance, they see that as an opportunity to learn more.

6. Is cautious in drawing conclusions; conclusions are based on data. These students are cautious about drawing conclusions when there are insufficient data to support those conclusions. They are able to suspend their judgment and do not leap to answers beyond what the data allow. Their conclusions or answers are clearly supported by what is known. There is an absence of emotionality or hot-headedness to their arguments.

7. Functions on his or her own initiative. When presented with a problem or a task, these students are able to rise to the occasion. They do not need constant support and help; they are unafraid to take the initiative, and they start work without help from others. They do not reveal any dependency behaviors, do not need to be told what to do at every step of the way, and have some pride in their own independence.

8. Embraces thinking as a means of solving problems. These students value thinking as a means of solving problems and as a way to inform their decisions. They want to think for themselves; they want to think their own ideas, and they value the power that thinking brings to their lives. These students are independent and self-initiating and do not have to depend on others to be told what to do.

9. Is open to self-evaluation; is nondefensive in self-evaluation. These students see self-evaluation as a means of learning more about themselves as learners. Their nondefensiveness allows them to see themselves more objectively and identify where they need help. They welcome the opportunity of engaging in a self-evaluative process.

Behaviors Related to Thinking Skills

10. Gathers and organizes data intelligently. When given an assignment to do research, to gather information about certain topics, these students are able to locate what they need, use more than one source, extract what is important in the material, and organize it in a way that makes sense. They do not resort to copying whole pieces of information in their entirety; they understand that doing research means finding out and making one's own sense of what has been discovered.

11. Gives examples in support of ideas. These students are able to give examples to support a particular point of view. The examples they give are appropriate and lend support to their ideas. They are able to make intelligent connections between the ideas and the examples that support them.

12. Generates hypotheses that are reasonable and an appropriate means of addressing a problem. These students are able to look at a problem and suggest some relevant and appropriate possibilities that would lead to solving that problem. Their suggestions make sense and represent intelligent explanations of how to go about finding solutions. There is a close connection between what the problem poses and their suggested guidelines for action toward solution.

13. Makes intelligent interpretations of data. These students are able to read, listen to, or observe information and draw intelligent meanings from what they have read, heard, or seen. The interpretations they make are based in the data; they do not jump to conclusions when there is insufficient evidence. They do not distort the data to support their own ideas, and there is a close match between what they say and what the data allow.

14. Differentiates between opinion and fact, between assumption and fact. These students are very clear about the differences between their opinions and facts and between what they assume to be true, and what is, in fact, true. When talking about their opinions, they use qualifying words to suggest their uncertainty. When they are presenting an argument, they indicate when they are sure (stating facts) and when they need to be cautious (stating an opinion or making an assumption) in their reasoning. Their arguments are strengthened by factual support rather than by personal belief and speculation.

15. Makes evaluative judgments that are based on appropriate criteria. These students are able to make sound judgments that are based on relevant criteria. They identify the criteria by which their judgments are being made, and the evaluative comments represent critical examination of how the qualities of the product meet or fail to meet the articulated standards.

16. Makes thoughtful, intelligent choices with respect to problems, ethical issues, and moral dilemmas. These students have clear belief systems, and their beliefs guide their decisions in problem solving and in deciding where they stand on ethical issues and moral dilemmas. They have reflected on what is important to them, and their beliefs have been chosen in relation to those value positions. There is a clear relationship between their beliefs and their actions.

LAST WORDS

The profiles presented in this chapter depart from the common classroom practices of marking and grading *how much* students know and, instead, put the emphasis on the ways in which student thinking is reflected in their behavior in a variety of learning situations. As this book has pointed out in several chapters, thinking is a process—as in, for example, "mental health," that cannot be assessed as a "fixed condition." The way we think is represented in our actions, in the way we deal with the day-to-day problems, events, and issues that we face and that confound us. The most important way we can judge how we think is through the way we behave in dealing with those problems, issues, and events. Observing and analyzing that thinking-related behavior is a powerful indicator of how well and the extent to which those processes are in operation.

Like other systems of assessment, the profiles as tools are fallible. But they will, at the very least, represent the teacher's best professional judgments, based on observations over time, of how a student is performing on those tasks that require higher-level mental functioning—the best and most informed method of student assessment.

When push comes to shove, it is the classroom teacher who makes the ultimate, bottom-line decisions about what happens in a classroom. From what I have written above, it is clear that I believe that teachers, more than anyone else, *have* that right. But I also believe that teachers make those bottom-line decisions based on what they consider to be imperative for the health, well-being, and educational development of their students—for what teachers believe ultimately guides and informs their every classroom decision.

In matters of the "what" and the "how" of teaching, teachers will decide for themselves whether and to what extent they consider building intelligent habits of mind a matter of urgency for today's and tomorrow's youth. And if in their judgment they choose for thinking, it is my earnest wish that they be gifted with the kinds of results that have encouraged and inspired teachers in the past to make critical thinking an overall objective of school life.

References

Adam, M., Chambers, R., Fukui, S., Gluska, J., & Wassermann, S. (1991). *Evaluation materials for the graduation program*. Victoria, BC: Ministry of Education.

Bloom, B. (1956). *Taxonomy of educational objectives, handbook I: Cognitive domain*. New York: McKay.

Bracey, G. W. (1998). Minds of our own. *Phi Delta Kappan, 80*(4), 328-329.

Bransford, J. D., Brown, A. L., & Cocking, R. R. (Eds.). (2000). *How people learn: Brain, mind, experience, and school*. Washington, DC: National Academy Press.

Carkhuff, R. (1969). *Helping and human relations: Volume II*. New York: Holt, Rinehart.

Costa, A. (Ed.). (1985). *Developing minds: A resource book for teaching thinking*. Alexandria, VA: ASCD.

Christensen, C. (1995, April 20). A community of learners. (1995). [Interview]. *Harvard Gazette*.

Coghlan, A. (2004, May 16-22). Will designer brains divide humanity? *NewScientist, 2708*, 8-9.

Education Commission of the States. (1982). *The information society: Are high school graduates ready?* Cited in Christie, K., Stateline: Premature arrival of the future, *Phi Delta Kappan, 89*(3), 165-166.

Flanders, N. (1970). Interaction analysis. In *Analyzing teacher behavior*. Reading, MA: Addison Wesley.

Freire, P. (1983). *Pedagogy of the oppressed*. London: Continuum.

Gleick, J. (1992). *Genius—The life and science of Richard Feynman*. New York: Vintage Books.

Gleick, J. (2000). *Faster: The acceleration of just about everything*. New York: Vintage Books.

Gough, D. (1991). *Thinking about thinking*. Alexandria, VA: NAESP.

Grant, N. (2000). *Oxford children's history of the world*. New York: Oxford University Press.

Green, E. W. (2006, October 22). Heeding a teaching moment. *U.S. News & World Report*.

Greenhouse, S. (1966, December 25). The child labor issue ignites a multifaceted youthful crusade. *New York Times*.

Goldberg, J. (2008, July-August). My amygdala, my self. *Atlantic, 302*(1), 96-100.

Gould, S. J. (1981). *The mismeasure of man*. New York: Norton.

Kozol, J. (2005, December). Confections of apartheid: A stick-and-carrot pedagogy for the children of our inner city poor. *Phi Delta Kappan, 87*(4), 265-275.

Kridel, C., & Bullough, R. V. (2007). *Stories of the 8-year study: Re-examining secondary education in America.* Albany: State University of New York Press.

Kristof, N. D. (2008, January 27). The age of ambition. *New York Times*, p. 18.

Lewis, A. (2007). Looking beyond NCLB. *Phi Delta Kapan, 88*(7), 483–484.

Parsons, T. (1971). *Guided self-analysis.* Unpublished manuscript, University of California, Berkeley.

Paul, R. & Elder, L. (2002). *Critical thinking: Tools for taking charge of your learning and your life.* Saddle River, NJ: Pearson.

Pogrow, S. (2005). HOTS revisited: A thinking development approach to reducing the learning gap after grade 3. *Phi Delta Kappan, 87*(1), 64–75.

Raths, L. E., Wassermann, S., Jonas, A. & Rothstein, A. (1966). *Teaching for thinking: Theory and application.* Columbus, OH: Charles Merrill.

Raths, L. E., Wassermann, S., Jonas, A., & Rothstein, A. (1986). *Teaching for thinking: Theory, strategies, and activities for the classroom.* New York: Teachers College Press.

Segal, J. W., Chipman, S. F., & Glaser, R. (1985). *Thinking and learning skills, volumes 1 and 2.* Hillsdale, NJ: Lawrence Erlbaum.

Shapiro, B. (1994). *What children bring to light.* New York: Teachers College Press.

Sternberg, R. J. (1987). Teaching critical thinking: Eight easy ways to fail before you begin. *Phi Delta Kappan, 68*(6), 456–459.

Thomas, H. (1995). *The first humans: The search for our origins.* London: Thames and Hudson.

Vialou, D. (1996). *Our prehistoric past.* London: Thames and Hudson.

Wassermann, S. (1987). Teaching for thinking: Louis E. Raths revisited. *Phi Delta Kappan, 68*(6), 460–466.

Wassermann, S. (1993). *Getting down to cases.* New York: Teachers College Press.

Wassermann, S. (1994). *Introduction to case method teaching: A guide to the galaxy.* New York: Teachers College Press.

Wassermann, S. (2000). *Serious players in the primary classroom.* (2nd ed). New York: Teachers College Press.

Wassermann, S. (2004). *This teaching life: How I taught myself how to teach.* New York: Teachers College Press.

Wassermann, S., & Eggert, W. (1976). Profiles of teaching competency. *Canadian Journal of Education, 1*(1), 67–93.

Wassermann, S., & Ivany, J. W. G. (1996). *The new teaching elementary science: Who's afraid of spiders?* New York: Teachers College Press.

Wassermann, S., & Wigmore, J. (2000). *Presumed enemies.* [CD-ROM] Vancouver: Figaro Educational Software.

Wilgoren, J. (2001, June 6). Repetition rap = charter school success. *New York Times*, p. B7.

Index

Adam, M., 198

America's Promise, 3

Answers: and keys to productive discussions, 19, 22-23, 24; "right"/definitive, 19, 22, 24, 35. *See also* Responses

Applying knowledge/information: and asking questions, 36; and guide to thinking activities, 46, 52; for language arts activities, 118-19, 121, 124-25, 126-27, 129, 132, 135, 138-40, 142, 144-45, 147-48, 150-51; for mathematics activities, 55, 57, 59, 61, 63-64, 66, 68-69, 71-72, 73-74, 76, 78, 80; and planning for teaching for thinking, 45; for science activities, 82-83, 85, 87-88, 90-91, 93-94, 96-97, 100, 102-3, 105-6, 108-9, 111-12, 114-15; for social studies activities, 154, 156-57, 159-60, 162-63, 166, 168, 171-72, 174, 176-77, 179-80, 182-83, 186. *See also* Decision making; Imagination/creation; Principles; Problem solving; Project design

Appreciation, showing, 19, 21

Art, 48-49

The Art of Storytelling (Grades 3-7), 136-40

Asking Good Questions (Grades 3-7), 140-42

Association of American Colleges and Universities, 3

Assumptions, 11, 201

Attending, 19-20, 26, 38, 40

Attitudes, 35, 189, 197, 200

Behavior: and attitudes about thinking, 200; control of, 189-91; evaluation of thinking-related, 198-202; maladaptive, 11; as means for determining extent of thinking, 51-52; patterns in, 198; profiles of thinking-related, 198; related to quality of thinking, 199-200; related to thinking skills, 201-2; and standards of performance in thinking, 196; and thinking theory, 9-11

Belief systems, 202

Big ideas: and asking questions, 30, 32, 34-35, 40; "big," 45; debriefing the, 194; and evaluation of student progress, 199; examples of, 44; and guide to thinking activities, 43-45, 52; identification of, 32, 44, 45; and keys to productive discussions, 19; for language

arts activities, 116, 120, 122, 125, 128, 130, 133, 136, 140, 143, 146, 149; for map study, 17; for mathematics activities, 53, 55, 57, 60, 62, 64, 67, 70, 72, 74-75, 77, 79; purpose of, 44; for science activities, 81, 83-84, 86, 88, 92, 95, 98, 101, 104, 107, 110, 113; for social studies activities, 152, 155, 158, 161, 164, 167, 169, 172, 175, 178, 181, 184; sources for, 32, 44; as too limited, 45; and well-orchestrated discussions, 40

Bloom, B., 25, 33

Body language, 20

Bracey, G. W., 7, 196

Brain-mind research, 50-52

Bransford, J. D., 51

Brown, A. L., 51

Bullough, R. V., 4

Carkhuff, R., 25

Chamber, R., 198

Chipman, S. F., 11

Christensen, C., 20, 192

Clarification; asking for, 20-21

Climate, classroom, 19, 20, 26, 35, 40, 189, 191, 192

Closure, 19, 22-23, 194

Cocking, R. R., 51

Commission on Behavioral and Social Sciences and Education, 51

Communicating Clearly (Grades 3-7), 130-33

Comprehending, 19, 20-21

Computer studies, 48-49, 50

Conducting Investigations Using Computers to Calculate (Grades 3-7), 79-80

Conformity, 4-5

Control; by teachers, 189-91

Costa, A., 11

Creating Drama (Grades K-7), 143-45

Creative thinking. *See* Imagination/creativity

Curriculum: and application of thinking theory, 14; and guide to thinking activities, 45-46, 50-52; Play-Debrief-Replay, 45-46; and teaching for thinking in a curriculum framework, 9-14; teaching strategies as connecting with, 11; thinking as integral to every, 11; thinking as vehicle for learning the, 46

About the Author

Selma Wassermann is professor emerita in the faculty of education at Simon Fraser University, Vancouver, Canada. She has taught in elementary schools in New York and California, as well as at Newark State College (Kean University) and Hofstra University. A recipient of the University Excellence in Teaching Award, she has published widely. Among her publications are six Teachers College Press books: *Serious Players in the Primary Classroom: Empowering Children Through Active Learning Experiences*; *The New Teaching Elementary Science: Who's Afraid of Spiders?* (with George Ivany); *Teaching for Thinking: Theory, Strategies, and Activities for the Classroom*, second edition (with Louis E. Raths, Arthur Jonas, and Arnold Rothstein); *Getting Down to Cases; Introduction to Case Method Teaching: A Guide to the Galaxy*; and *This Teaching Life: How I Taught Myself to Teach*. She lives in Vancouver with her husband, Jack.